PLASTICUS MARITIMUS
An Invasive Species

PLASTICUS MARITIMUS
An Invasive Species

Ana Pêgo

Bernardo P. Carvalho

Isabel Minhós Martins

Translated by Jane Springer

DAVID SUZUKI INSTITUTE

GREYSTONE KIDS

GREYSTONE BOOKS • VANCOUVER/BERKELEY/LONDON

First published in Canada, the U.S., and the U.K. by Greystone Books in 2020
First paperback edition published in 2021
Originally published in Portuguese in 2018 as *Plasticus maritimus, uma espécie invasora*
Text copyright © 2020 by Ana Pêgo and Isabel Minhós Martins
Illustrations copyright © 2020 by Bernardo P. Carvalho
Translation copyright © 2020 by Jane Springer

22 23 24 25 26   6 5 4 3 2

Greystone Books Ltd.
greystonebooks.com

David Suzuki Institute
219 – 2211 West 4th Avenue
Vancouver, BC V6K 4S2

Cataloguing data available from Library and Archives Canada

ISBN 978-1-77164-645-1 (pbk)
ISBN 978-1-77164-643-7 (cloth)
ISBN 978-1-77164-644-4 (epub)

Editing by Patricia Aldana
Copyediting by Rowena Rae
Proofreading by Dawn Loewen
English text design by Belle Wuthrich
Cover illustration by Bernardo P. Carvalho

Printed and bound in China on FSC® certified paper by Shenzhen Reliance Printing

Greystone Books thanks the Canada Council for the Arts, the British Columbia Arts
Council, the Province of British Columbia through the Book Publishing Tax Credit,
and the Government of Canada for supporting our publishing activities.

Canadä

Greystone Books gratefully acknowledges the xʷməθkʷəy̓əm (Musqueam),
Sḵwx̱wú7mesh (Squamish), and səl̓ílwətaʔɬ (Tsleil-Waututh) peoples on
whose land our Vancouver head office is located.

Contents

Introduction

My beach (and how it explains a lot of things)

I'm a marine biologist. I'm not sure when I first began to have a preoccupation with plastics. There probably was no exact moment when I had a sudden insight. I don't even remember if it took place on what I call "my beach," though that would seem most likely.

My beach is only 650 feet (200 meters) from the house where I grew up. It is a special beach because it has a rocky area that creates lovely tide pools. At low tide, these pools full of sea water are a refuge for a huge variety of animals and plants.

Some people have a yard behind their house. I was lucky enough to have a beach two minutes away, the most incredible backyard anyone could have. At low tide, the smell of the sea was amazing and so strong that it wafted up the street to my house.

Every day, I'd arrive home from school, throw my backpack into a corner, and call into the house, "Mom, I'm going to see how the beach is doing!" And I'd head off. Going to the beach was like going to visit a friend to get a sense of how they were feeling.

I've always loved studying tide pools. See how beautiful they are!

Though I didn't really realize it, going to check out the beach meant spotting a lot of different things:

- Whether the tide was high or low (or was coming in or going out)
- Whether the sand was the same as the day before or had changed (sand accumulates in different parts of the beach depending on the seasons and the tides)
- Whether the sea was calm or choppy
- Whether there was anyone else on the beach or I had it to myself

A.

Montagu's crab,
or furrowed crab
(*Lophozozymus incisus*)

B.

Snakelocks anemone
(*Anemonia sulcata*)

C.

Spiral wrack alga
(*Fucus spiralis*)

D.

Purple sea urchin
(*Paracentrotus lividus*)

E.

Dog whelk
(*Tritia incrassata*)

F.

Limpet
(*Patella* sp.)

On days when the tide was low, there was a path between the rocks to the next beach, and along the way, I picked up fossils or looked at the marine animals.

Now, I also pick up the garbage I find scattered on the beach.

My obsession with marine plastic resulted from a combination of different things. But the time that I spent in the water pools on my beach probably explains it best. It was there that I learned to love the sea. And when you love something, the most natural thing is for you to care about everything that's related to it.

Why focus on ocean plastic?

There's a long list of problems related to the oceans. Here are some examples:

- Increase in water temperature owing to climate change
- Problems related to overfishing
- Sound pollution caused by maritime traffic
- Chemical pollution (often invisible) coming from diverse sources, such as oil spills or untreated sewage
- Animals and plants in trouble and needing help to survive

I chose ocean plastics because they represent 80 percent of the garbage in the oceans. All evidence points to a relationship between the presence of microplastics in the oceans and numerous health problems in both animals and humans. Algae, fish, and many other species are affected. And it is clear that humans are already suffering the consequences of contamination by this invasive species, ocean plastic.

Lots of problems need solutions

One positive thing about the time we're living in is that we have a good understanding of the problems that need to be solved. This is a big advantage over other periods in history when there was less communication worldwide and when science was much less advanced. Today, if we care about the planet and about everyone who lives here, we can have a better understanding of what's going on. Scientists study the problems and gather information and in many cases have already come up with solutions—and this is an enormous advantage. But things are not always resolved, are they?

That's true, first, because there's a huge array of problems to sort out; second, because even though the information exists, it doesn't always reach people; and third, because people, institutions, or governments don't all have the same priorities or are not doing their jobs the way they should.

This is why it is very important for us to take an active role. Being an activist means precisely this. If there's a problem that we're troubled by, and if we can see that this problem has serious consequences, then we need to recognize it and get down to work to change the situation.

The world can only move forward if we don't wait for these problems to be resolved on their own or for others to resolve them.

It doesn't matter how old we are, what our occupation is, or whether we think we're on our own. There are all kinds of examples of people worldwide, people of all ages and backgrounds, who have become spokespersons for a cause. And there are also many examples of one person making a difference.

This book aims to turn you into a specialist in ocean plastic. It contains the basic information you need to have a good understanding of the problem so that together we can confront it in the best and most effective way.

In this book

This book begins with a discussion of the role of the oceans in the life of the planet. It looks at how plastic is produced and describes the consequences that plastic garbage has for life on earth. It explains why I have decided to give ocean plastic a scientific name—*Plasticus maritimus*—and call it an invasive species.

The field guide to ocean plastic presents examples of the most common types of ocean plastic as well as the most exotic types I have come across. Throughout the book, you will hear about what people are doing to combat ocean plastic and how you can get involved.

I hope this book will encourage you to get to work: to refuse to use plastic that is unnecessary, to look for alternative solutions, to be inspired by the ideas that you encounter, and to come up with your own ideas. There are already many of us working on this issue, but we need an ever-growing network of people in order to get rid of the plastic in the oceans. Join us!

Has it always been like this?

Almost everything around us is made of plastic or of materials that contain some plastic. Today, we can live in a house with plastic floors and furniture, work on a plastic table with computers made of plastic, dress in plastic clothes (check the labels, you'll be amazed), put on plastic shoes, eat food that comes packed in multiple layers of plastic, and eat and drink with plastic plates and cups. In many countries, even some toothpastes and face and body scrubs or exfoliants have plastic in them.

It's normal to use plastic. So normal that we don't even think about it. But it hasn't always been like this. Today, we live a life of buying, using, and throwing away, a life that was unthinkable to people a hundred years ago. We have access to a huge quantity and variety of consumer goods and we are used to products that last for a short time.

Many of the things we use come in packages. Packaging is useful because it protects products, enables their transport, and provides information about them. However, it is common for products to be overpackaged to make the products look larger. In addition, products are often placed inside large polystyrene packages that are unnecessary. This is the case of the prepackaged fruit, vegetables, and meat that we buy in supermarkets.

It doesn't make sense to return to the past, to the time when milk was transported from the countryside to the cities by horse and buggy. We've invented amazing things in the meantime and it would be foolish not to make the most of the technologies and materials that exist.

Yet it's important to think about the consequences of our choices and decide when to buy or use something made of plastic. It may be a unique and useful material, but it has such huge impacts on the environment that we must use it consciously.

This cellphone is a dinosaur.
It's already four years old!

The Importance
of the Oceans

What the oceans mean to us

We don't always remember, but the oceans have three very important functions in the life of the planet: they are the main regulator of climate, they produce more than half of the oxygen that we breathe, and they are the habitat and source of food for huge numbers of living things.

THE PLANET'S THERMOSTAT

A thermostat is a device that regulates temperature. The oceans act as a kind of planet thermostat. They absorb and store a large part of the sun's radiation and prevent the earth's temperature from getting too hot. In addition, the oceans' currents redistribute the sun's heat to different regions. This helps to maintain the comfortable temperatures we have on earth and makes it possible for humans to live here.

THE PLANET'S LUNGS

When we talk about oxygen, the first thing we think of is trees or forests. What we might not know is that plants in the ocean are responsible for more than half of the oxygen we breathe. There is a huge mass of microscopic plants called phytoplankton or microalgae. We're unaware of them because they are so small you can only see them through a microscope. They are floating around the oceans and doing exactly what all other plants do. Through photosynthesis, they absorb carbon dioxide and produce oxygen.

If the oceans were to become full of plastic and pollutants, this mass of microalgae would quickly disappear. That could happen because the toxic substances in plastic kill some of the microalgae, and also because huge amounts of plastic floating around make it difficult for the sun's light to penetrate the water. Without sunlight, microalgae die.

AWESOME NUMBERS

An astounding 50 to 70 percent of the oxygen we breathe is produced in the oceans. In fact, the oceans produce more oxygen than all of the rainforests together. (This does not mean that rainforests are not essential. Long live the rainforests!)

A huge thank-you to microalgae.

Without them, we wouldn't be here.

THE OCEAN FOOD CHAIN

In the ocean food chain, the smallest organisms are eaten by larger ones. The chain begins with phytoplankton or microalgae, the microscopic plants that float around the oceans.

1. Phytoplankton are the base of the food chain and serve as food for many animals.

2. Next in line are zooplankton, the tiniest-sized animals (such as fish larvae or minuscule crustaceans) that serve as food for small fish.

3. Next come the medium-sized fish, and then the giant ones. We humans are also part of the ocean food chain.

We know that some phytoplankton adhere, or stick, to microplastics in the sea. If the phytoplankton are the base of the ocean food chain, you've already figured out what will happen next— all the animals that feed on phytoplankton will be eating plastic. And all the animals that eat the animals that eat the phytoplankton will also be eating plastic! That includes us.

For the planet to be healthy, the ocean's phytoplankton must be healthy, because they begin the nutrient cycle that feeds an enormous number of living beings on earth.

The interaction between humans and oceans

A lot of memorable things have happened between us and the oceans: expeditions, discoveries, problems, and decisions. Here are some of the most important.

1872–1876
The British Challenger expedition circles the earth, bringing new information about ocean temperatures, currents, marine life, and the sea floor.

1943
Jacques Cousteau and Émile Gagnan create the Aqua Lung, the first underwater breathing device, making extended underwater exploration and filming possible.

1950
Plastic waste begins to reach the oceans.

1960
A guided probe reaches the bottom of the Mariana Trench, the deepest point on the ocean floor, about 36,000 feet or 11,000 meters down.

1970
Scientists issue the first warnings about the existence of microplastics in the North Atlantic.

1973
The International Convention for the Prevention of Pollution from Ships—the MARPOL Convention—is signed. It restricts discharges of waste (including plastics) from ships.

1992
The Topex/Poseidon satellite begins mapping the surface of the oceans.

1995
The Geosat satellite begins mapping the bottom of the oceans.

1997
While taking part in a regatta, Captain Charles Moore discovers a huge island—of plastic—in the North Pacific Ocean. He is one of the first people to draw attention to the ocean plastics problem.

2008
The United Nations (UN) creates World Oceans Day—June 8.

2010
The first census (or official count) of marine life takes place, examining the diversity and distribution of marine animals, plants, and fungi.

Organizations from all over the world begin to publish guidelines to combat the marine garbage problem.

2011
Plastic industries commit to taking action to help solve the problem of plastics in the oceans.

2012
Marine garbage is one of the priorities of the UN Conference on Sustainable Development (Rio+20).

2014
The word "microplastic" enters our everyday vocabulary.

2016
France becomes the first country in the world to pass a law banning the use of disposable plastic that is not biodegradable.

The UK approves a law to ban microplastics in cosmetics.

2018
The European Union (EU) presents its plastics strategy: by 2030, all packaging in EU countries must be recycled or reused.

2019
British scientists begin to map ocean plastics by satellite.

2020
More people and countries all over the world become aware of the ocean plastics problem. If you are reading this book, you're part of this group!

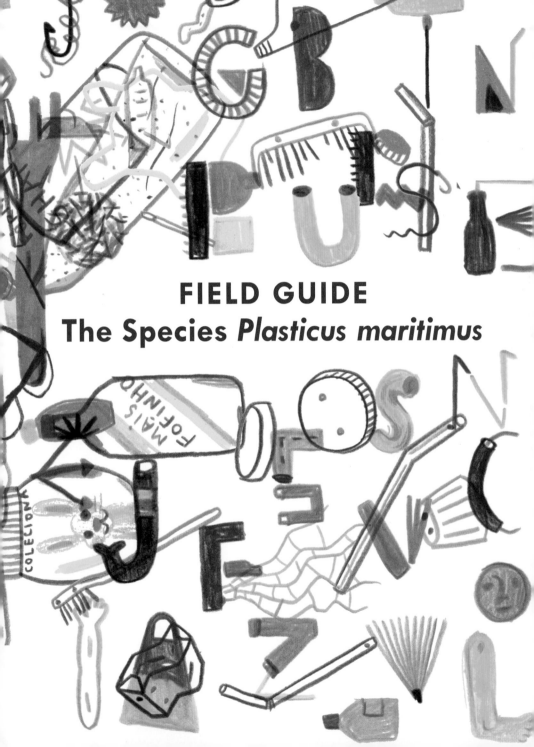

FIELD GUIDE
The Species *Plasticus maritimus*

A species that doesn't exist...but here it is

This field guide aims to help us understand a species that doesn't belong to the natural world but that has become common on our beaches and in our oceans—ocean plastic. When I came across it more and more, I thought it was important to give it a scientific name. After all, things become more real to us when we name them and give them an identity.

Inspired by the terminology that scientists use, I invented a name for this species: *Plasticus maritimus. Plasticus* because it is a species made of plastic and *maritimus* because it can be found in all seas and coastal areas worldwide. I classified it as an invasive species—that is, a species that is not native to the place where it's found and causes harm in the new environment.

Plasticus maritimus is invasive wherever it appears.

WHY SUCH COMPLICATED SCIENTIFIC NAMES?

As you may have noticed, scientific names are always designated in Latin and are composed of two words written in italics. It's not just to make things more complicated and important-sounding. It's to ensure that every species has its own name and that we don't confuse two different species of plants or animals.

We all know the common names of some plants and animals. But these common names are different in different countries and even in different regions of the same country. So, for example, the scientific name helps clear up any doubt when you call a particular wild flower a devil's paintbrush and your friend insists it's an orange hawkweed. When you look in your wildflower field guide, you find you're both right. This wildflower has many common names. But the scientific name for the plant is *Hieracium aurantiacum*. The field guide also tells you that the wildflower that you found in British Columbia is originally from southern and central Europe.

The scientific name allows us to observe in detail the aspects that scientists study when they are examining a particular species. Scientists want to determine the family to which a species belongs; its characteristics, including its life cycle; and where it's found on the planet—whether in a particular region or in many regions.

For example, *Tursiops truncatus* (common bottlenose dolphin) is the name of a species of dolphin that has a resident population in the Sado estuary in Portugal. But in the Azores, Portugal, a species called *Delphinus delphis* (short-beaked common dolphin) is more widespread. They're both dolphins, but they're two distinct species.

The name of a species is made up of

1. a generic or genus name (always begins with a capital letter), and

2. a specific or species name (always written in lowercase letters).

Plasticus maritimus

Together, these two terms identify the species and avoid big misunderstandings.

Some species, including this one, also have subspecies. In this case, the subspecies name differentiates between common versions of the species (*Plasticus maritimus vulgaris*) and those that are more rare (*Plasticus maritimus exoticus*).

What species is this?

IDENTIFICATION SHEET

Scientific name:

Plasticus maritimus (Pêgo, 2015)

This is the name of the scientist who identified the species. That's me, Ana. My surname is Pêgo.

This is the year in which the species was identified.

Family: Plasticidae.
This is the family of species that possess some type of plastic in their constitution.

Characteristics: This species appears in a wide variety of forms. Usually, these forms are identifiable—we can easily recognize a fishing net or a water bottle. However, *Plasticus maritimus* often turns up in unfamiliar ways. In these cases, we can't tell what the object is and we must investigate.

Color: *Plasticus maritimus* can be any color, including an undetectable color. That is, it may be transparent or appear in such small particles that it's impossible to see what color it is.

Dimensions: This species can be found in all sizes from very large to very small and is sometimes even invisible to the naked eye.

Means of movement: In general, *Plasticus maritimus* moves easily and rapidly depending on the winds and currents. The lightest examples fly and float but heavier ones may remain a long time at the bottom of the sea.

Distribution: This species is found in all of the world's oceans and coastal areas.

Imitative abilities: *Plasticus maritimus* is a champion at mimicry. It can change itself to look like animals. For example, it can imitate jellyfish that are food for turtles. It can also make itself so small that it mixes in with and is mistaken for plankton.

Adaptability: This species adapts easily to all ecosystems and demonstrates great tolerance for differences in temperature and salinity. This is why, over the last fifty years, its population has increased exponentially and in an uncontrolled manner, affecting all marine and coastal habitats in the world. *Plasticus maritimus* integrates so well into our lives that we don't even notice it. As a result, it is an extremely dangerous species.

Life cycle: The first phase of the life of *Plasticus maritimus* is on land, so it is confused with the species *Plasticus terrestris* (meaning land-dwelling). The age at which it passes into the aquatic environment is variable. It may happen after a few minutes, a few days, or many years of terrestrial life. Its arrival in the ocean may happen directly or indirectly, in which case it passes first through streams, rivers, or other waterways.

Toxicity: Toxicity is generally high, but it is variable. The most toxic forms are those with additives that make this species softer, or more flexible, or more long-lasting. There are also pollutants in the oceans that adhere to the surface of plastics during their stay at sea.

Endemic/exotic/invasive: Not endemic (not naturally occurring in a certain area); an exotic and invasive species.

Conservation status: Currently, there are no threats to *Plasticus maritimus*. It is a threat itself!

Eradication: The greatest threats to the existence of *Plasticus maritimus* would be to eradicate disposable plastic products (at present 50 percent of plastic is used only once), reduce the production and consumption of plastic products, and increase reuse and recycling of plastic products.

Plasticus maritimus is on the list of exotic invasive species that threaten the biodiversity of the oceans and our existence. Its eradication is urgent! If you come across any, pick it up and put it in a plastics recycling bin, if possible, or a garbage container.

How much plastic is in the sea?

An American scientist named Jenna Jambeck was the lead author of a big research study to find out how much plastic goes into the oceans every year. Making these calculations is not easy, so it took a large team of scientists from many different fields. The study concluded that every year, about 9 million tons (8 million metric tons) of plastic ends up in the oceans. Almost all of it is packaging!

This is equivalent to about 1,000 tons (900 metric tons) of plastic being dumped into the sea every hour. Every single minute, that's a truckload full of plastic, without stopping.

The most recent estimates also indicate that with population growth and the increase in plastic consumption, this number will double by 2025. This is how we come to the sad conclusion that by 2050, there will be more plastic in the sea than fish.

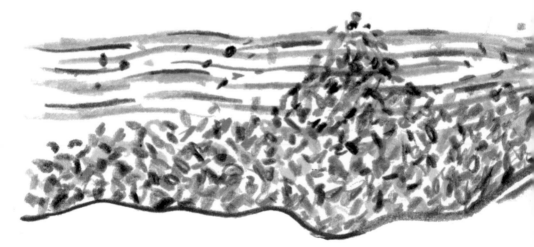

Nine million tons (8 million metric tons) of plastic ends up in the oceans every year.

Where does the plastic go?

We might think that the plastic ends up in the most populated parts of the world or near the coast, but that's not the case. There is plastic scattered all over the oceans of the whole planet. You find it even in the most remote regions, such as in the Arctic (North Pole) and on isolated islands of the Pacific.

What we see on our beaches is just the tip of the iceberg. Not only is there plastic floating in sea water, but massive quantities of it have accumulated on the ocean floor.

Plastic doesn't float forever, and after a while, due to algae or animals clinging to it, it gets weighted down to the bottom. It's the same thing that happens when a plastic carton fills with water and becomes so heavy that it no longer floats.

Christopher Kim Pham, a scientist at the University of the Azores, Portugal, is one of the authors of a study that aimed to find out where the plastic goes and how much there is on the ocean floor in European coastal waters.

The study was carried out at thirty-two sites in the Atlantic Ocean and the Mediterranean Sea. It found plastic on the ocean floor in all these locations. There was even plastic in places 1,800 miles (3,000 kilometers) from the coast, in the middle of the Atlantic, and sometimes at great depth!

As Pham said, "The plastic got there before we did!"

How long does it take for plastic to decompose?

The decomposition time of plastic depends on many things: the type of plastic, the size of the piece, the environmental conditions (sun exposure, water temperature, currents), and the areas it has passed through or where it is found. For example, the plastics that end up on the ocean floor take a long time to decompose because of lower water temperatures and the fact that they are in low-light and less-eroded areas. In theory, because plastic is an organic (carbon-containing) material made from petroleum, it should eventually break down into carbon dioxide and water. But no one knows how long this will take, because no one has lived long enough to see plastic disintegrate completely.

ESTIMATED TIME IT TAKES FOR
OCEAN LITTER TO DISINTEGRATE

Plastic straw: 200 years

Soft drink can: 200 years

Disposable diaper: 450 years

Plastic bottle: 450 years

Fishing line: 600 years

WHAT IS BIODEGRADABLE?

Biodegradable materials are those that break down due to the action of bacteria and other organisms, leaving nothing except for carbon dioxide and water (i.e., substances that exist in nature).

Plastic decomposes very slowly and can take many centuries to completely disappear.

The consequences of plastics in the oceans

When fish, birds, turtles, whales, and other species come across plastic in the oceans, it is almost always an unhappy encounter. There are three especially worrying situations:

1. When animals ingest plastics or microplastics that accumulate in their organs and tissues.

2. When animals are trapped and/or injured in nets, plastic loops, or other objects.

3. When plastics release the additives in their chemical makeup and the pollutants they have adsorbed from the sea.

*Ad*sorption is different from *ab*sorption. Here, adsorption refers to how the molecules of a pollutant cling to the surface of a plastic.

Heartbreaking images

The internet and documentary films about the oceans often show shocking images of animals that have suffered the effects of plastic. It's hard to forget these images.

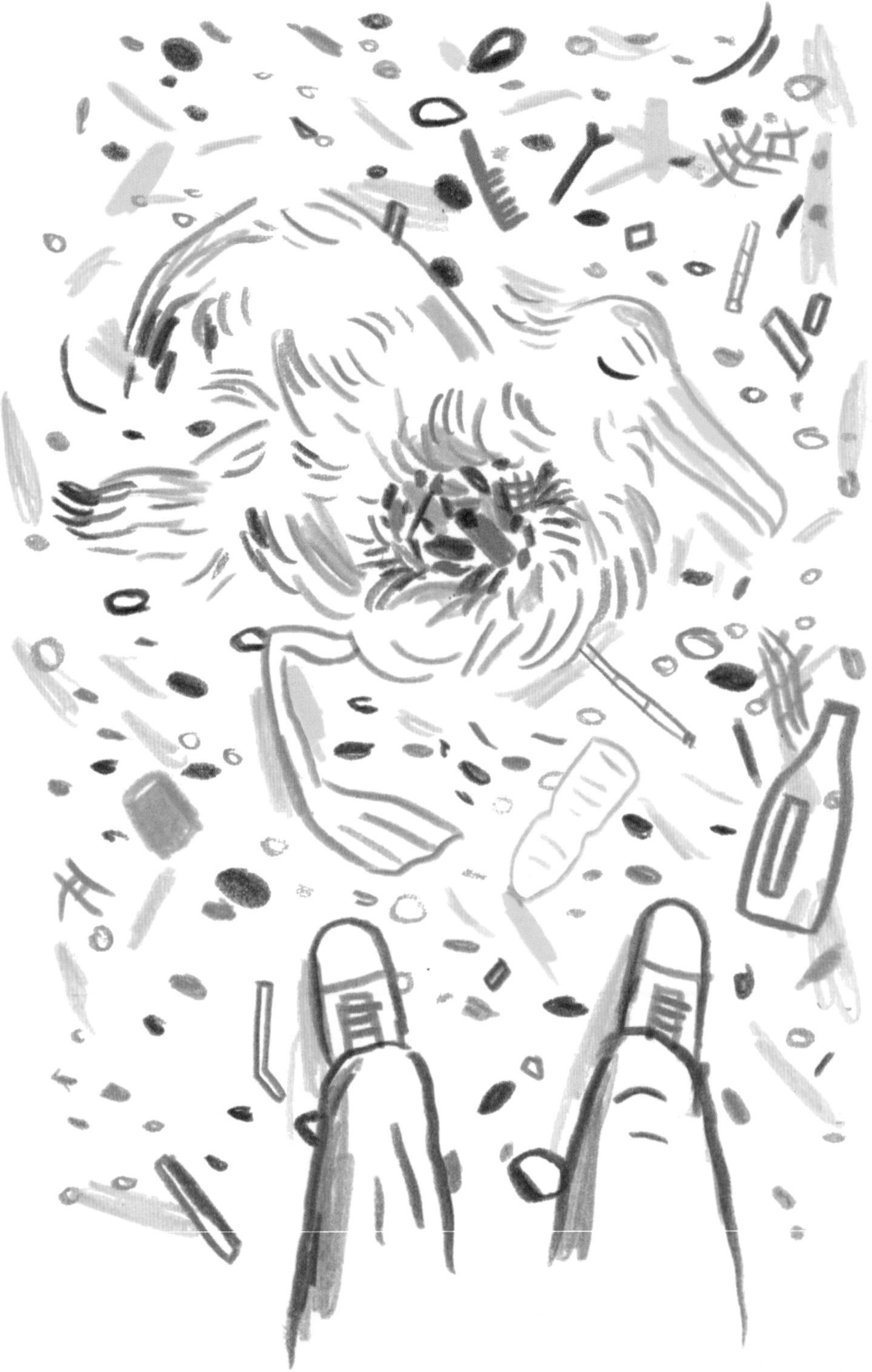

1. Photographer Chris Jordan took photos of albatross chicks on Midway Island in the Pacific Ocean. They show the effects of a plastic-based diet fed to them by their parents. They did not survive. How does something like this happen?

It's simple. The colors and shapes of plastic attract the albatrosses and other animals. And when plastic has been in the sea for a long time, it may be covered in algae or tiny animals and smell like tasty food. Albatross parents easily confuse it with food and, full of good intentions, collect it to feed their offspring. After a short time, the chicks die.

Many animals that ingest plastic end up dying of hunger. Why? Because even though the plastic fills up their stomachs and makes them feel full, they haven't really eaten. So they die of starvation.

2. In 2017, a sick goose-beaked whale was beached on a shore west of Bergen in Norway. It died. Thirty plastic bags were removed from its stomach during the necropsy (an autopsy of an animal). In 2018, a pilot whale washed ashore in Thailand with eighty bags in its belly!

3. There are equally alarming images of turtles whose shells have grown deformed inside a plastic loop used to link up drink bottles or cans.

4. Turtles often mistake plastic bags for jellyfish. As jellyfish are one of their favorite foods, the turtles don't think twice about eating the bags—and then they die.

5. There are countless cases of animals injured from pieces of sharp plastic. Their wounds may be external or internal (when they are ingested or when a plastic object enters a body opening).

6. Animals become entangled or trapped in fishing nets lost at sea or stuck in pieces of plastic packaging. Unable to move, they cannot come to the surface to breathe or find food. Often, a dead animal in a net attracts predators that end up trapped in the net as well.

At the University of the Azores, scientists have been monitoring sea turtles and Cory's shearwaters, seabirds that breed in the Azores archipelago. They found that 80 percent of the turtles and almost 90 percent of the birds studied contained plastics in their digestive systems.

The toxic nature of plastic

Plastic has very particular chemical characteristics. It is a material capable of adsorbing other substances. Plastic that has been around for a long time at sea almost always contains large amounts of pollutants. That's because molecules of liquid pollutants adhere to its surface. These pollutants may be old chemicals that have somehow ended up in the sea. Many of them have been banned, but they are still in the water.

Plastic also has the ability to release substances that are part of its own makeup. Prolonged exposure to heat causes some plastics to release their additives as well as the pollutants they have adsorbed. One group of additives that has been proven to be very harmful to human health is phthalates (pronounced THAL-ates).

Some plastics contain a huge amount of toxic substances. Even when the plastic biodegrades into very small particles, these toxic substances are still present. Once the particles with toxins have entered the food chain of ocean animals, they pass into human tissue through the fish and shellfish we eat.

Microplastics are a macroproblem

As it drifts all over the oceans, plastic suffers damage from cold, heat, sun, salt, waves, wind, and contact with sand and rocks. It gradually becomes weak and breaks down into thousands of small particles. Plastic particles less than one-fifth of an inch (5 millimeters) long are called microplastics.

SOME EXAMPLES OF MICROPLASTICS

▸ Bits of plastic or objects that have become fragmented

▸ Microbeads, the tiny balls of plastic present in creams and body scrubs or exfoliants (abrasive compounds that supposedly make the skin smoother). Microbeads are produced on purpose in minute sizes. They don't dissolve, and when they are rinsed down a drain, they can end up in rivers and lakes and eventually the ocean.

▸ Resin pellets or nurdles (small pellets or beads) that serve as raw materials in the production of plastic objects

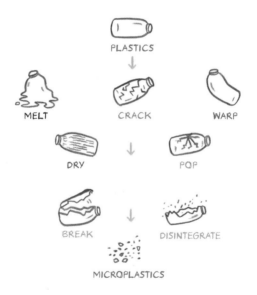

PLASTICS

MELT   CRACK   WARP

DRY   POP

BREAK   DISINTEGRATE

MICROPLASTICS

Despite their "micro" size and almost always being invisible to the naked eye, these small pieces of plastic are a serious problem. Not only is it impossible to extract them from the oceans, but they are ingested by small marine organisms and affect all living things along the food chain, including humans.

And so?

We don't yet know all the effects on humans of ingesting micro-plastics. We do know that in some marine organisms, microplastics can be incorporated into tissues and cause inflammation and damage to cells. In addition, microplastics often contain chemicals added during the production of the plastic and pollutants that exist in the seas—the so-called persistent organic pollutants (POPs), such as PCBs, PAHs, and DDT.

PCB is the abbreviation for a product group called *p*oly*c*hlorinated *b*iphenyl; PAH stands for *p*olycyclic *a*romatic *h*ydrocarbon; DDT is the abbreviation for an insecticide, *d*ichloro*d*iphenyl*t*richloroethane. Some of these chemicals have been banned, but they continue to circulate in the oceans.

These products can concentrate in the tissues of living things, mounting up with time, in what is called bioaccumulation. Pollutants also become more concentrated at ever higher levels of the food chain. They can cause serious health problems, and particularly affect the endocrine system (which regulates the glands that secrete hormones), causing changes in growth and reproduction.

WHAT'S WITH BIOACCUMULATION?

Bioaccumulation is the process by which toxic substances accumulate and continue to accumulate in living organisms. Pollutants and additives may be bioaccumulating in marine organisms and, as a result, reaching humans through our diet.

Plastic garbage patches

Plastic tends to collect in the ocean's gyres—large circular ocean currents that are like huge whirlpools. When plastics go into a gyre, they're pulled into the center where they form a huge mass called a "garbage patch." There are five garbage patches—in the North Atlantic, the South Atlantic, the North Pacific, the South Pacific, and the Indian Ocean. The largest is the Great Pacific Garbage Patch located between Hawaii and California.

The "plastic islands" in the oceans should in fact be called "plastic soups." Almost all the plastic pieces (95 percent) in the seas are smaller than a grain of rice.

The 5 Gyres Institute, an American organization, arranged twenty-four expeditions to the five oceans. They returned with an estimated 5.25 trillion pieces of plastic that had been drifting in the oceans!

What about plastic in lakes, rivers, and streams (*Plasticus lacustris*)?

Some plastic gets dumped directly into the oceans, but most of it is carried there by rivers and streams. In fact, rivers act as a kind of conveyor belt, moving ever larger amounts of plastic and shifting it steadily downstream into the oceans.

Towns and cities have always been built on rivers, and some rivers now run through heavily populated areas. But even many modern cities don't have good waste collection, recycling systems, or sewage systems. That means a lot of plastic ends up in local rivers, and from there it flows downstream into the ocean.

Not all the plastic makes it to the ocean, of course.

There are large and small pieces of plastic in lakes and rivers, just as there are in the oceans. We don't know as much about the effects of macroplastics on freshwater mammals, fish, reptiles, and crustaceans as on their ocean cousins. But we are starting to recognize the effects of having microplastics in fresh water. That is because we drink fresh water.

A 2017 study found microplastics in 83 percent of tap water tested from around the world. The highest concentrations were in North America. Bottled water, most often sold in plastic bottles, had an even higher rate of microplastics—93 percent—in a 2018 study.

Plastic isn't just a problem in the oceans—it's a problem in fresh water all over the globe.

The case of the North American Great Lakes

The Great Lakes make up one-fifth of the surface fresh water on the planet. And they provide the drinking water for about 40 million people in Canada and the United States.

An estimated 10,000 tons (9,000 metric tons) of plastic enters the Great Lakes every year (photo of Lake Erie).

As in the oceans, a lot of the plastic sinks to the bottom of the lakes, where it will continue to affect life of all kinds for many years to come. But unlike the ocean plastic that collects in ocean garbage patches, lake plastic collects on or near the lakeshores. That's because the Great Lakes currents are not as strong as the ocean gyres, the large circular currents that trap ocean plastic. In the lakes, winds tend to break up any accumulated debris and deposit it close to shorelines instead.

That makes floating lake plastic easier to clean up than the plastic in the ocean garbage patches. But the shoreline is also where drinking water is taken from—and a place inhabited by wildlife. And the Great Lakes water eventually makes its way to the sea.

PLASTIC IN THE SOIL (*PLASTICUS TERRESTRIS*)

Scientists are beginning to study plastic pollution of the soil and its impact on plant growth and terrestrial ecosystems as a whole. They estimate that there is at least four times more plastic on land than in the oceans.

Plastic gets into the soil as compost or other soil amendments, as a part of sewage that is treated and then used as fertilizer, as litter, and in rainwater, floodwater, or road runoff.

A 2019 study found that earthworms placed in soil with large amounts of plastic lost weight. It's clear we have a lot to learn about the effects of plastic on agricultural production. But that's another story—and another book!

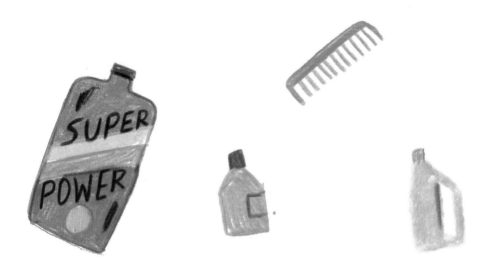

Do You Want to Know More about Plastic?

What's so special about plastic?

Plastic is a synthetic material. It is lightweight, flexible, and durable and can be produced in a wide variety of densities, shapes, textures, transparencies, and colors. Because it is so versatile, it allows us to enjoy objects that are not only beautiful, but well adapted to our needs. For example, thin and delicate plastics are used to make tights or contact lenses. More durable plastics are used to make artificial skin. Some plastics resistant to chemicals are used for packaging toxic detergents. There are plastics so strong that they are used in bulletproof vests, planes, and cars.

Because it doesn't degrade easily, plastic is an obvious choice for objects that have a long life. But why do we need to use such a strong and durable material for things that are only in our hands for a few minutes or a few hours?

That's the big question.

Flexible

ONE WAY PLASTIC BENEFITS THE ENVIRONMENT

Many means of transport, such as cars and planes, contain a lot of plastic. Because plastic makes them lighter, these means of transport need less fuel to operate than those made of other materials.

Resistant

Lightweight

IS IT REALLY NECESSARY?

A plastic bag has an average use time of only fifteen minutes—but a life of hundreds of years ahead of it.

What about the glasses, plates, cutlery, lids, and straws you use when you're eating lunch in a shopping center restaurant?

Even if it takes you a long time to eat, the life span of this disposable plastic will be, at most, fifty or sixty minutes.

BRIEF HISTORY OF PLASTIC PRODUCTION

1856: Parkesine, the first semisynthetic plastic, is invented. It is made from cellulose and nitric acid. (Cellulose is the chief substance found in the walls of plant cells.) Billiard balls, which used to be made of ivory, are now made of this material. Inventor: Alexander Parkes.

1907: Bakelite, the first totally synthetic plastic, is invented. Unlike Parkesine, which was made from natural materials, Bakelite is artificial, a hard plastic used for making radios and telephones. Inventor: Leo Baekeland.

1913: Polyvinyl chloride (PVC) patent is registered.

1916: The first cars with plastic interiors appear.

1930s: New plastics like polystyrene and polyethylene emerge. People are simply amazed...

1938: The first toothbrushes made of polyamide (nylon) appear.

1941: A patent is registered for polyethylene terephthalate (PET), a new lightweight plastic.

1948: The first vinyl long-playing records (LPs) are produced.

1949: The first plastic-fiber fabrics are sold.

1950: The first plastic bags appear.

1950s: Plastic objects are mass produced. Plastic products like radios and home appliances are cheaper and more affordable. The race to the shops and the plastic begins!

1953: German Hermann Staudinger wins the Nobel Prize in Chemistry for demonstrating the existence of macromolecules, which he calls polymers (for more information, see page 58).

1955: Many countries, such as the United States, portray disposable consumption as a feature of sophisticated modern living. Using something once and throwing it away is chic!

1957: Polypropylene (PP) comes into the market.

1958: Lego registers a patent for its famous interlocking plastic bricks.

1976: Plastic becomes the most widely used material in the world.

1979: The first mobile phones—made of plastic, of course—are introduced.

1989: The first plastics that emit light are created.

1990: The first biodegradable plastic is sold (finally!).

2000s: Nanotechnology enters the world of plastics.

2009: The Boeing 787, made with 50 percent plastic material, makes its first flight.

2019: Sandra Pascoe Ortiz, a Mexican engineer at the University of the Valley of Atemajac, discovers a way to turn cactus leaves into a material that has properties similar to plastic. She says it's not toxic and it's biodegradable.

In spite of huge efforts by environmentalists, plastic production soars. The production and disposal of plastic uses almost 14 percent of all the oil and gas in the world.

2020: Environmentalists continue to fight the petrochemical industry over plastic production.

More governments and corporations commit to a reduction in the production of plastic at a UN oceans conference in June in Portugal.

Quick class in physics and chemistry

WHAT IS PLASTIC, ANYWAY?

All plastics are synthetic materials—that is, they've been created by humans. They belong to a large family of materials called polymers.

Polymers are very large molecules (macromolecules) and are made up of smaller units called monomers that bind together, forming long chains.

Think of a necklace of beads or a daisy chain in which an element repeats, and repeats, and repeats. A polymer looks like this under a microscope.

When the repeated chemical element is always the same, it is called a homopolymer (e.g., the polyethylene in some plastic water bottles). When the chemical elements in a chain vary and form different sequences, it is called a copolymer (e.g., the PVC in some detergent packaging).

In order to be a polymer, the monomer that makes it up has to be repeated at least 10,000 times!

homopolymer　　　　　　　　　　　　　　**copolymer**

NOT ALL PLASTICS ARE THE SAME

There are two large families of plastics: thermoplastics and thermosets. The main difference between them is based on their relationship to heat.

Thermoplastics	Thermosets
Low melting point	High melting point
Can be remelted and recast into various shapes	Stay in solid state; chemical structure changes when reheated
Easier to recycle	Difficult to recycle
Examples: PVC (polyvinyl chloride), PS (polystyrene), and PE (polyethylene)	Examples: polyurethane foams and Bakelite

How plastic is produced (in six steps)

1. The main raw materials used in the manufacture of plastics come from the petrochemical industry, from oil. Oil is a complex mixture of thousands of chemical substances, many of which are hydrocarbons (i.e., compounds that contain only carbon and hydrogen).

2. Crude oil is heated in a refinery. It is subjected to high temperatures (up to 750 degrees Fahrenheit, or 400 degrees Celsius) so that the elements that make it up—the derivatives—separate. This separation happens because the derivatives condense (become liquid) at different temperatures.

3. After the crude oil is heated, it's pumped into a distillation tower. The crude oil vaporizes and rises up the tower. The different oil derivatives condense at different levels of the tower. The heavier molecules of asphalt, bitumen, and tar stay at the bottom while the lighter molecules of naphtha, diesel, gasoline, and aviation fuel rise to the top.

4. Once distilled, the simpler mixtures of hydrocarbons, called fractions, are used for making different types of plastic. Ethylene, the simplest substance used in making plastics, is obtained from naphtha. Gasoline is used to produce petrochemicals such as propylene, butadiene, and styrene.

5. The fractions are turned into plastic through a process called polymerization (a chemical reaction that makes polymers). Some polymers are made by linking hydrocarbon monomers together into long chains. Others are made by a more complex process called condensation polymerization.

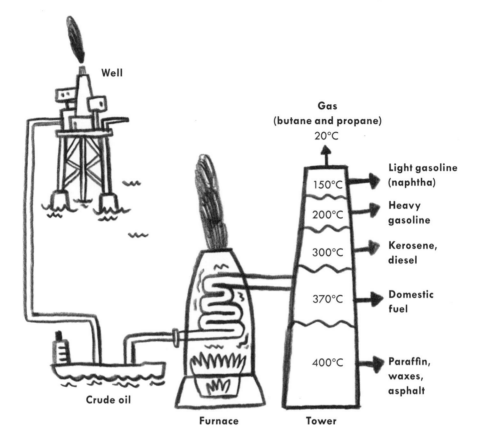

Well

Gas
(butane and propane)
20°C

150°C → Light gasoline
(naphtha)

200°C → Heavy
gasoline

300°C → Kerosene,
diesel

370°C → Domestic
fuel

400°C → Paraffin,
waxes,
asphalt

Crude oil

Furnace   **Tower**

Note: 20°C = 70°F, 150°C = 300°F, 200°C = 390°F, 300°C = 570°F,
370°C = 700°F, 400°C = 750°F (values are rounded)

6. Once the plastic is produced, it is common to add other
ingredients to alter its characteristics. These might be a
coloring substance, something that increases flexibility or
prevents disintegration in heat or sunlight, or a filler made of
minerals that makes the finished plastic cheaper.

WHERE IS PLASTIC PRODUCED?

Plastic is made all over the world. Half of the world's plastic is produced in Asia (29% China, 4% Japan, and 17% the rest of Asia); 19% in Europe; 18% in North America; 7% in the Middle East and Africa; 4% in Latin America; and 2% in the Commonwealth of Independent States (Russia and eight other countries).

Plastic in nature

You might have noticed that it's very common to use the word "plastic" in a negative sense, to designate something that is artificial and that should not exist.

But in nature, there are also natural polymers that have been used for a long time. This is true of the resins of some trees and insects; bitumen; and the waxes, shells, and horns of some animals.

ENVIRONMENTAL CONSEQUENCES OF PLASTIC PRODUCTION

Environmental impacts occur early in the processes of oil extraction and during transport of the oil, if accidents lead to oil spills.

During the distillation of oil, large quantities of carbon dioxide and other gases are released that increase the greenhouse effect of the planet. In other words, whenever oil is distilled, the process contributes to climate change.

Common Ocean Plastic

Everyday objects:
Plasticus maritimus vulgaris

Every day, at all hours, waves bring in garbage to the beaches.
In 2018, more than one million volunteers in 122 countries took
part in the International Coastal Cleanup sponsored by the Ocean
Conservancy. They collected 23.3 million pounds (10.5 million
kilograms) of ocean garbage. Here are the Top Ten types of waste
collected worldwide, all made of plastic:

1. Cigarette butts
2. Food wrappers
3. Straws, stirrers
4. Forks, knives, spoons
5. Beverage bottles
6. Bottle caps
7. Grocery bags
8. Other plastic bags
9. Lids
10. Cups, plates

WHERE DOES SO MUCH GARBAGE AND SO MUCH PLASTIC COME FROM?

We might think that marine garbage comes just from beaches or walkways next to beaches. But it may come from far away. For example, it can

● blow in from a garbage can,
● reach the sea via a river or other waterway, and
● come through the sewers of our houses.

Four-fifths of marine debris originates from activities that take place on land. One-fifth originates from activities at sea, including fishing, passenger ships, fish farming (aquaculture), and offshore oil drilling rigs or platforms.

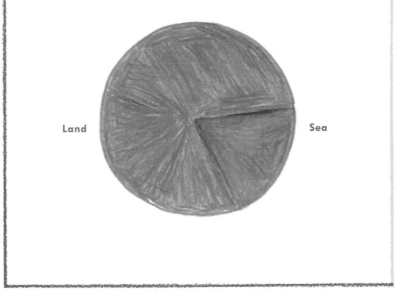

Land   Sea

What you'll find

Many plastic objects are extremely common on our beaches. Here are the ones you're most likely to find.

CIGARETTE BUTTS

Butts are the champions of marine debris. It is estimated that 4.5 trillion butts are tossed on the ground worldwide each year. There is still no plan to recycle cigarette butts in most countries, so they should be deposited in the garbage, rather than on the ground.

Origin: Cigarette butts are often flung directly into the sea or thrown into the toilet. But even if they are chucked onto roads and sidewalks or into gutters or streams, the butts find their way into waterways and to the sea with the help of rain or road cleaning.

Characteristics: We tend to think that cigarettes are made of paper, but they contain plastic in the filter as well as toxic substances that are harmful to ocean health, as well as to the health of those who smoke. Cigarette butts take between one and five years to break down.

Tip: Always wear gloves to pick them up.

COTTON SWABS

Origin: Many people flush cotton swabs down the toilet, never imagining that they could end up in the sea.

Characteristics: Thin plastic tubes of varying colors. They usually appear without the cotton tip, so they are often confused with lollipop sticks.

Distribution: They are most often found on sandy beaches, but many get stuck in the rocks on rocky beaches.

FOOD PACKAGING

Origin: Packages are "forgotten" at a picnic site on the beach, they fly out of garbage bins or recycling areas, or they are pulled out of bins by animals.

Characteristics: They show up on beaches in all shapes and conditions. Some examples: yogurt and ice cream cartons; potato chip, lozenge, and candy bags; cracker and cookie packaging.

Hazards: Many of these packages cannot be recycled at all or are very difficult to recycle (see Recycling, page 123, for more information).

WATER BOTTLES, CAPS, AND RIMS

Disposable water bottles have only been around for about sixty years, but they have quickly become central to our lives. About 20,000 water bottles are bought every second worldwide, but only 7 percent of them are recycled. Each of these bottles contains a cap and a small rim, which when they are loosened, are unlikely to be recycled.

Caps and rims show up in the thousands in all colors, from transparent to black. The most common ones are probably the blue ones from small and large water bottles.

Origin: Sidewalks, beaches, parks, waterways.

Decomposition time: Estimated to be 450 years!

A good idea: Some companies are trying to find a way to keep the caps on the bottles after they've been opened. This would prevent so much plastic being let loose everywhere!

Once, on a walk in Cabo Raso,
I found 253 lids in just 20 minutes!

FISHING NETS AND ROPES

Origin: Commercial and recreational fishing vessels and boats, ports, beaches.

Characteristics: Nets, ropes, and other materials used in fishing are made of plastic, mainly of nylon monofilament and nylon polyfilament.

Hazards: Many of these materials—called "ghost gear"—are lost for years at sea. They cause the entanglement and death of many animals. Over time, fishing nets and ropes break down into microfibers that enter the food chain.

A good idea: Some companies have begun to use lost nets to make new products, from swimming suits to jeans.

PLASTIC BAGS

Origin: They reach the sea via waterways or by flying out of garbage bins.

Characteristics: In the ocean, they look like jellyfish, so turtles eat them.

Interesting fact: In 2018, a thin plastic shopping bag was found at the bottom of the Mariana Trench, the deepest place on earth.

A good idea: There are bans on plastic bags in sixty-nine countries, and thirty-two countries have imposed a charge per bag. The problem is most countries have only partial bans and no countries restrict the production of plastic bags.

POLYSTYRENE (STYROFOAM)

Origin: The takeout food market uses vast numbers of Styrofoam containers. Many fishers use polystyrene blocks to make buoys or bait boxes. It is also used for packaging household appliances and as insulation.

Characteristics: It is very light, flies around, floats, and breaks up into thousands of pieces and tiny balls.

Hazards: It is common for animals to mistake these "little balls" for eggs of other species and eat them!

Good ideas: Some companies are beginning to replace Styrofoam used in packaging appliances with cardboard.

RESIN PELLETS OR NURDLES

Resin pellets are plastic particles used in manufacturing large plastics. Both preproduction and recycled resin pellets, also called nurdles, are used to produce all kinds of plastic objects. Unfortunately, it is possible to find them on almost every beach in the world.

Origin: There are leaks during production or while transporting the pellets to the factories that produce plastic objects. Leakages also occur during cleaning of the places where the pellets are produced or handled.

Characteristics: They are small granules of plastic resin (normally under one-fifth of an inch, or 5 millimeters, in diameter). They go unnoticed because they look like pebbles or grains of sand.

Hazards: Many animals ingest them, because they confuse them with eggs of other animals.

Interesting fact: Beachcombers call them mermaid's tears!

Cases that deserve attention

THE BALLOON WAR

Some people like to release balloons to celebrate important dates. They may even do it to draw attention to a problem, which means they had good intentions. But balloons eventually come down from the sky. They can be blown long distances by the wind and fall into the ocean.

In 2007, French people in Normandy were surprised to see balloons arriving at their beaches on the occasion of Queen's Day, a popular festival in the Netherlands. The balloons had traveled 500 miles (800 kilometers).

Birds swallow pieces of balloons or get entangled in the wires or strings. They die from suffocation or hunger because they can't move.

Now many of the drifting balloons are fitted with small LED lamps. They look beautiful, but imagine what happens when the batteries of the LEDs (and the substances they contain) fall into the sea, along with the balloons.

What to do?

Aside from the balloons used by meteorologists, balloons are not essential in our lives. The best practice is to do without them. Second best is to collect them after their use and throw them into the garbage.

Note: Biodegradable (natural rubber) balloons do not solve the problem, because they can last for three or four years outside and can also cause damage to the environment.

In just one day, I found 133 plastic straws on my favorite beach.

FLYING STRAWS (NOT ALWAYS CHARMING)

In 2015, two scientists studying sea turtles in Costa Rica saw a turtle that was having trouble breathing. After observing it, they found that a plastic straw was stuck in its nostril. The scientists filmed the attempt to remove the straw and shared the video on social networks. The film went viral, and since then, more and more people around the world have decided to say no to straws.

Straws are not essential. Apart from people who need to use them because of illness or disability, we can live perfectly well without them. They are one more part of the family of disposable objects whose fleeting, one-time use consumes a huge amount of raw material and energy.

The straws are made of plastic that is not always recycled. And they are often wrapped in a plastic covering that, like the straws themselves, is very lightweight. Because they are so light, straws and their packaging often fly off outdoor patios and out of garbage cans and end up in a waterway on its way to the sea.

It may be fun to use a straw once in a while, but that's not what's happening. In Europe alone, it is estimated that 36 billion straws are consumed every year.

What to do?

Most of the time we can easily do without straws. When we do wish to use them, there are metal, bamboo, or paper alternatives. Many portable metal cutlery kits also contain metal straws.

Exotic Ocean Plastic

Rare finds:
Plasticus maritimus exoticus

When we spend time on a beach, we don't just find common plastic objects, like the ones we talked about in the last chapter. Anyone who walks with their eyes focused on the sand will one of these days find some rare specimens, some of them very mysterious.

These exotic objects travel in time and space. Their history is important because it offers a better understanding of the movement of plastic in the oceans and gives us information about its decomposition. But it is not always easy to identify these pieces—to know what they are, where they come from, or how long they have been at sea. In these cases, the internet is useful, because it puts people from all over the world who are interested in this subject in contact with each other. I'm part of a worldwide network of people who help each other identify objects that crisscross the oceans and, every once in a while, land on shore.

A FANTASTIC NETWORK OF
WORLDWIDE IDENTIFICATION

My Facebook page for *Plasticus maritimus* allows me to keep in touch with beachcombers from all over the world and to help identify the material that lands on coasts worldwide. One of the great managers of these lost-and-found objects is Tracey Williams from England, creator of the "Newquay Beachcombing" and "Lego Lost at Sea" projects. By connecting people from all over the world, Tracey has made a huge contribution to helping identify many objects.

Exotic objects

Object: Bait jars for crab and shrimp fishing
Place: Several beaches near Cascais, Portugal, and
on Faial Island, Azores
Dates: 2016–2019

These bait jars are from the United States and Canada. They are
used inside crab and shrimp traps.

The day I took this picture, I found two jars and two lids, all in
different places. Since then, I've come across many, many more.

Object: "Destiny" buoy
Place: Arriba Beach, Cascais, Portugal
Date: May 5, 2016

This buoy with the mysterious inscription "Destiny" had some barnacles attached to it. That meant that it had been roaming the ocean for a long time.

But where did it come from? And how long had it been wandering the ocean?

I uploaded the photo onto my *Plasticus maritimus* Facebook page and it crisscrossed the world and brought me an answer back.

A lot of theories came up, but none was convincing. The image was shared with an online beachcombing group, and eleven days later, an American named Aaron Soares wrote a message. Aaron was on the New Jersey swordfish and tuna fishing boat that the buoy came from. The distance from New Jersey to Arriba Beach is about 3,390 miles (5,450 kilometers)!

Object: Russian Navy emergency water pouch
Place: Abano Beach, Cascais, Portugal
Date: June 10, 2016

I found a water bag with an inscription in both Russian and English. It said "Emergency Drinking Water." It was a packet of water used in the Russian Navy's lifeboats, in case sailors needed to abandon ship.

Object: Can of Chinese cigarettes called "Double Happiness"
Place: Cabo Raso, Cascais, Portugal
Date: June 18, 2016

I found a can of Chinese cigarettes. When I opened the lid, the tin was full of cigarette butts. When I put the photo on my Facebook page, people from other countries responded saying they'd found cans of the same brand with butts inside. A number of theories were proposed, but no one knew the origin of the cans. It seems clear that sailors used the cans as ashtrays and then tossed the cans overboard rather than putting them in a garbage can.

Object: Single-colored toys
Place: Various beaches near Cascais
and the Alentejo coast, Portugal
Dates: 2016 and 2017

The first time I found one of these dolls, I was intrigued, and
then I found another, and another, and another. It seemed to be a
collection, but what was its history? And how long ago had it been
produced? I found out that these dolls were produced in the 1960s
and 1970s and offered as gifts for people who bought various
brands of European ice cream. These dolls still show up
on the beaches of Cascais.

Object: Regurgitations from gulls and other seabirds
Places and Dates: Crismina Beach (March 4, 2016)
and Conception Beach (March 15, 2016), both in Portugal

Some seabirds (including gulls) have the ability to regurgitate what
they cannot ingest (such as shells and crab claws). Therefore, they
usually manage to expel the microplastics we see in the photos.
But not all birds have this ability, and so the plastic they eat
accumulates inside their bodies.

When I published these photos on social networks, I was contacted
by Laurent Colasse, a researcher from the French Research
Institute for Exploitation of the Sea (IFREMER), who asked me
to send him all my regurgitation photos. Laurent works with the
Dutch ornithologist Jan Andries van Franeker on an international
research project that studies pellet pollutants (microplastics) and
the impacts of their ingestion by seabirds. The research focuses
particularly on the northern fulmar, or Arctic fulmar (*Fulmarus
glacialis*), which has become an indicator of plastic pollution in
Northern Europe.

Object: Lobster fishing trap tag
Place: Several beaches near Cascais, Portugal,
and on Faial Island, Azores
Dates: 2016 and 2017

In the United States and Canada, lobster traps have a tag
indicating the fishing license number, authorized fishing area,
year, and country of origin. Canadian Julie-Sophie Tremblay is
mapping Canadian tags that have appeared in other countries
to pressure the government to use alternatives to plastic.

A tip:

How do we know if an object has been at sea for a long time? Pay attention to the signs! Check to see if there are any living organisms attached to it. Look for algae, bryozoa (invertebrate moss animals), barnacles, or polychaetes (bristle worms).

Other mysterious objects:
Plasticus maritimus complicadus

ORANGE PIECES OF PLASTIC WITH
THE WORD "SEAL" ON THEM

In September 2015, "the case of the orange tabs" triggered a big discussion on the internet. But it wasn't until July 2016 that the mystery was solved. I was exhibiting my collections in a workshop and talked about this case. A few days later, a young man named Manuel Fernandes wrote to say that these plastic tabs are used to seal a plastic bottle of spray sunscreen. Manuel made the discovery by chance, after a trip to the beach where someone was opening one of these containers and had to break this protection tab.

DIABETES LANCETS

It took me a long time to identify these pieces. I thought they might be related to medical treatments, since they had a pharmaceutical trademark. But what were they for? And why would they be on the beaches?

One day when I had to go to the hospital, I took some samples with me. The nurses immediately identified them. These pieces are lancets used by people with diabetes to take a small blood sample for a blood glucose test at their homes. After they use the lancet, many people flush them down the toilet. Eventually, they end up in the ocean.

BEACH UMBRELLA ENDS

These pieces were tricky to identify, even though they are part of an object that's common during the summer months. I was dying of curiosity about them before a boy gave me the answer during a visit I made to a school.

He recognized the pieces as the ends of sun umbrellas that are buried in the sand or grass to fix them to the ground. Unfortunately, these pieces often stay buried when the umbrella is removed. It's only when summer is over and the first strong tides turn over the sand that they come to the surface. There were days when I found more than forty on the same beach.

Can you identify these objects?

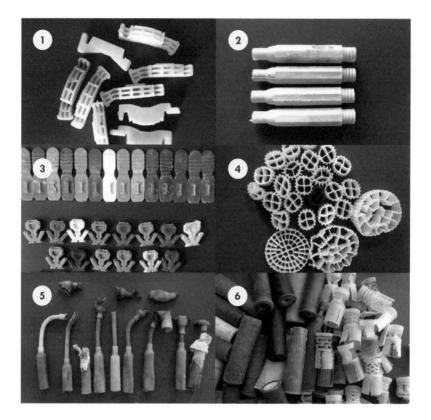

Solutions

1. Corners of fish transport trays (they create some space between trays and prevent the fish from getting crushed)
2. Still a mystery... do you have any ideas?
3. Pieces used to seal some kind of (unknown) boxes
4. Biological filters used in wastewater treatment plants
5. Parts of fireworks
6. Parts of shotgun shells

When shipping containers sink (with all the plastic they contain)

In 2017, some 130 million shipping containers were transported across the oceans. This is not surprising, considering that 90 percent of the products we consume (food, clothing, etc.) are transported by boat.

Once in a while, there are accidents and containers fall overboard. When they are locked or sealed, many containers float (and become a danger to navigation). Often, after colliding with rocks or boats, they open up, strewing their contents into the sea.

Every year between 2008 and 2016, an estimated 1,580 containers fell into the sea.

Here are some famous cases...

THE CASE OF THE CONTAINER CARRYING RUBBER TOYS, JANUARY 1992

Perhaps the best-known case is that of a ship carrying floatable rubber toys. During a big storm, a container of 28,000 of these toys fell overboard. There were blue turtles, green frogs, and red beavers, but the ones that became most famous were, without a doubt, the yellow ducks.

The ducks (and their friends) sailed along, following the currents. When they began to hit the shores, they were very useful to scientists.

Oceanographer Curtis Ebbesmeyer saw this wreckage as an excellent opportunity to learn more about the movements of ocean currents. He closely followed the journeys of the ducks and their friends.

Since then, the rubber ducks have been used not only to study currents, but as an indicator of how long it takes for a synthetic material like plastic to decompose at sea.

THE CASE OF THE CONTAINER CARRYING LEGO, FEBRUARY 1997

A cargo ship called *Tokyo Express* was hit by a massive wave in the sea off the coast of Cornwall, United Kingdom. The boat tipped so much to one side that sixty-two containers fell overboard. One of them contained five million Lego pieces, including many with nautical themes. The ironies of fate!

In no time, hundreds of miniature harpoons, fins, pirate swords, octopuses, and dragons (rare and greatly appreciated by beachcombers) began to arrive on the beaches of Cornwall's coast.

THE CASE OF HEWLETT PACKARD (HP) INK CARTRIDGES, EARLY 2014

In December 2015, through the Newquay Beachcombing internet page, I learned that a container had fallen overboard, probably in early 2014, dumping HP ink cartridges into the North Atlantic.

The news caught my attention because in September 2015, I had found an ink cartridge in Cabo Raso, Portugal. I contacted Tracey Williams, manager of the Newquay Beachcombing page, and sent her the reference number of the cartridge. As incredible as it seems, we confirmed that the cartridge that ended up on the Cascais coast was part of the shipment that fell into the North Atlantic.

I alerted the associations and groups that cleaned the beaches in Portugal and, in the first months of 2016, fourteen more cartridges were recovered just on the beaches near Cascais.

THE CASE OF THE PINK STAIN REMOVER, JANUARY 2016

A container of pink plastic bottles containing Vanish stain remover was dropped into the sea by a Japanese cargo ship called MV *Blue Ocean*. Thousands of bottles showed up on the coast of Cornwall, United Kingdom, alarming inhabitants and environmentalists. Nature conservation associations rushed to collect the bottles to prevent the toxic detergent from destroying the local marine fauna and flora. But it is likely that most of the bottles were lost and the noxious liquid they contained eventually leaked into the sea.

THE CASE OF THE KINDER SURPRISE EGGS, JANUARY 2017

This case also took place in January, the storm month in the northern seas. A Danish ship carrying containers between China and Germany was hit by Storm Axel and dropped five of its containers at sea. One of them contained thousands of Kinder Surprise eggs, each with a plastic toy inside it and a small sheet of assembly instructions in Russian.

The chocolate eggs came as a real surprise to the inhabitants of the small island of Langeoog, on the northeast coast of Germany. Children enjoyed picking up the hundreds of eggs on the beach, but the colorful scene wasn't so great after all—considering the huge amount of packaging materials that also turned up on their once-clean beaches.

How to Go into the Field

Plasticus maritimus, here we come!

Here, you'll find all the information you need to organize a biologist-style field trip. During this excursion you will be able to observe, collect, and identify some specimens of this menacing species.

Here are my tips for getting down to work.

I try to keep my backpack neat and tidy, but sometimes more important things come into play...

MATERIALS FOR COLLECTING LITTER

- Small bags
- Large, sturdy reusable bags
- Sieve (for microplastics)
- Bottles of various sizes
- Gloves
- Knife (very useful for cutting cables and fishing nets. It should only be used by adults or in the presence of an adult.)

When an excursion is planned, we can get the materials together ahead of time. But it is also important to be prepared to "hit the beach" at any time and collect plastic litter on the spot.

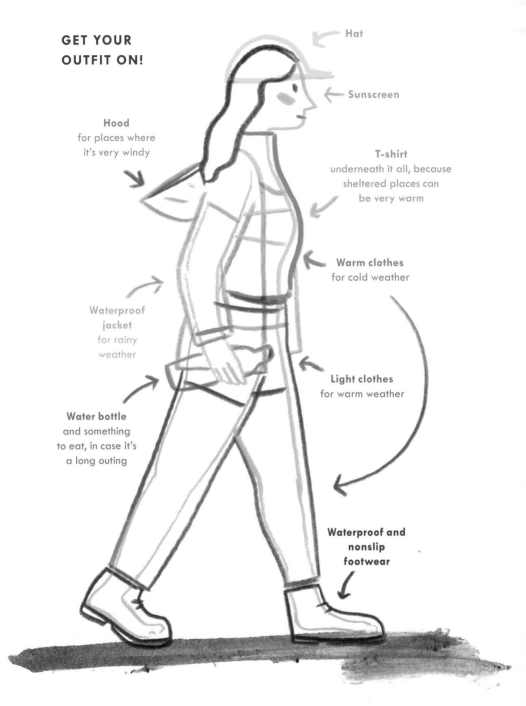

GET YOUR
OUTFIT ON!

Hat

Sunscreen

Hood
for places where
it's very windy

T-shirt
underneath it all, because
sheltered places can
be very warm

Warm clothes
for cold weather

**Waterproof
jacket**
for rainy
weather

Light clothes
for warm weather

Water bottle
and something
to eat, in case it's
a long outing

**Waterproof and
nonslip
footwear**

Don't forget to put sunblock on the back of your neck. You're always looking down at the ground, exposing parts of your body that are normally covered... (Yes, I've had a burnt neck and it wasn't fun!)

More tips

- Always have some bags in your backpack, in case you happen to be near a beach.

- Use a sieve or a strainer to separate the microplastics from the sand.

- When you know a place quite well, you can predict what you need to take. For example, if you are going to a place where there are large amounts of litter, take bigger bags.

Note: Children should always be accompanied by an adult. Walking and collecting litter by the sea is an activity that involves some risks.

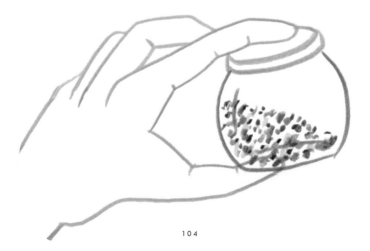

Things that sometimes happen when I'm at the beach

The battery runs out on my phone. (I get furious because I can't take photos or keep track of what I've found.)

I get hungry (sometimes so hungry that I can't think).

GRRAUU

I have to pee.

So before you leave, don't forget to

- go to the bathroom,
- eat,
- charge your phone, and
- bring a water bottle and a snack.

TWO RULES RELATED TO COLLECTING SPECIMENS

Although I don't pick up everything I find, I have two rules:

- If I grab something to see what it is, I always take it with me. That is, I don't put anything that I've picked up back on the ground.

- I focus on the objects that are most dangerous to marine life. This includes, for example, polystyrene foam (Styrofoam), because it crumbles into thousands of little balls, as well as plastic bags and fishing nets.

Beach alerts

It's very easy to be distracted when you're at the beach. It's important to be organized and alert to avoid accidents.

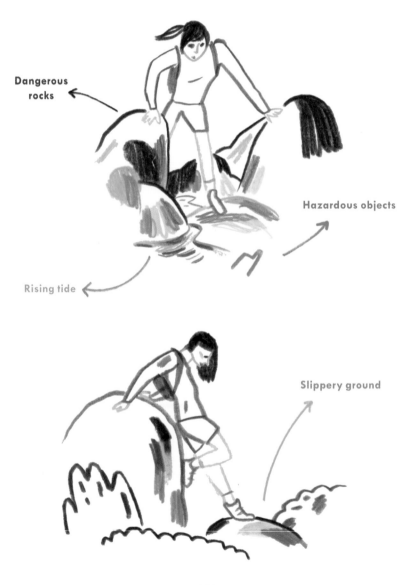

Dangerous rocks

Hazardous objects

Rising tide

Slippery ground

FIRST

It's important to remember that picking up garbage is not a joke.

BE CAREFUL COLLECTING GARBAGE

- There are sharp objects (such as glass and cans).
- There are objects that can prick (such as diabetics' needles and lancets for taking blood samples).
- There are very dirty and/or dangerous objects (such as bottles with strange liquids, packages covered with tar, and even dog poo).

SECOND

The sea can be dangerous. Pay attention to the changing tides and big waves, and be careful on days when the sea is rough.

SEA AND BEACH TIPS

- Always keep a good distance from the sea so you don't have to run to escape the waves.
- Take special care on beaches with lots of rocks and stones, where it is not easy to walk but easy to twist a foot.
- Keep in mind that algae are very slippery. Even those that you can hardly see can create a greenish film on the rocks and make them slimy.
- Remember that many people walk their dogs on the beach, so there can be a lot of disgusting poo in the sand. It's a drag to have to avoid these "mines," but it's a reality.

What you need to know about the tides

Tides are a result of the gravitational forces of attraction that exist between the moon, the sun, and the earth.

The earth attracts the moon and therefore the moon orbits around our planet. The moon also attracts the earth, but in a less obvious way. The continents are not affected, because they are solid masses, but the oceans, because they are liquid, feel this attraction.

The moon's force generates sea currents that cause two high tides and two low tides every day.

WHAT IS THE IDEAL TIDE?

The ideal for plastic collecting is to catch the tide as it's going out. It's easier not having to run from the waves. But also, when the tide is going out, it leaves behind interesting debris and sometimes even treasures.

I go to the beach whenever I feel like it, but if I know that the sea is very rough and strong, I avoid certain places or certain beaches.

TIDAL CYCLES

The tides operate in cycles of about six hours, alternating between high tide and low tide. Every day, there are two high tides and two low tides.

Each day, the tides "delay" by forty to fifty minutes—they happen forty to fifty minutes later than the previous day.

So, if today the low tide is at 12 noon, tomorrow the low tide will be at about 12:50 p.m.

High tide

Low tide

The best times

My favorite times to take walks and collect garbage on the beach are on days with bad weather, but not stormy days or days with a rough sea.

In the autumn, there are usually some spring or king tides (especially high tides), which bring a lot of garbage. Winter is a good season for marine debris, because there are strong winds that blow the debris onto the land and strong tides that help to dig up things trapped in the sand. But in very cold climates, it can be too cold to go out in winter.

For me, the least interesting time is summer, because many beaches are cleaned daily and the garbage that we find is recent. It's usually garbage that has flown out of crowded bins or been abandoned in the sand. In addition, the prevailing wind is less likely to blow garbage from the sea to the land during the summer.

I like to pick up marine garbage—garbage that has already journeyed by sea. If there's one thing I don't like, it's picking up fresh garbage! But sometimes you have no choice.

The best places

My experience tells me that the best places to collect microplastics are sandy beaches most exposed to the wind. For collecting large objects, I recommend less-frequented coastal areas and beaches that are hard to get to.

BEACH CLEANER OR BEACHCOMBER?

A beach cleaner is a person who cleans up beaches, as an individual or as part of a group. A beachcomber is someone who picks up litter from beaches, but not only that. A beachcomber is a sort of collector who is also interested in the origin and history of the objects they encounter. I am a beachcomber!

PS: I would be very happy if, while reading this book, readers become interested in going to the beach to pick up their own examples of *Plasticus maritimus*—and who knows, organize their own collection! Anyone who wants to can identify and post their findings on social media with the hashtag #plasticusmaritimus.

Funny things that happen to a beachcomber

When I'm picking up litter, it's only natural that I'm looking at the ground. Some people ask me directly what I'm doing: "Have you lost something?" or "Are you picking up shells?" Others watch me until they figure it out: "Ah! She's picking up plastic!"

New things show up every day and this makes the life of a beachcomber interesting. When I wake up, I ask myself, "What will I find today?"

There are days when certain things predominate—for example, certain objects or colors. Besides the "glove day" (when I found seven gloves in one morning), I had a "straw day" (when I collected 133 straws on the same beach), a "bottle caps day" (253 caps), a "white umbrella cones day" (40 cones), a "fishing buoys day," and a "cigarette lighters day."

There are also days when I say, "I'm sick of cotton swabs. I'm not picking up any today!" (It could be drinking straws or lighters.) But sometimes, after just a few minutes, I'm picking up cotton swabs anyway because there are so many of them. Or maybe the next day I am looking for those particular objects only. Nothing is certain in the life of a beachcomber...

ANYTHING VALUABLE?

I have never found a treasure chest full of gold coins or other valuable things. From time to time, I find a few coins, and I once found a €20 bill (about US$22 or C$30) just as I was leaving the beach. I treated it as a reward for the day's work.

What We Can Do

We can no longer say, "I didn't know..."

We're not always aware of environmental problems. This is the case with plastic in the oceans. Some people continue to use disposable plates and cups because they don't know that these objects can't always be recycled. In the same way, some people throw cotton swabs into the toilet, perhaps because it never crossed their minds that these objects would end up in the oceans. Surely everything would be different if everyone had access to information and knew the consequences of their actions.

It's true that it's been a relatively short time since plastics have become a problem and since people have begun to talk about it, so the information hasn't reached everywhere.

But those who know have to start acting and passing on the word, especially because the problem is getting worse.

WE DON'T WANT THIS TO HAPPEN, DO WE?

If no action is taken, it is estimated that by 2050, there will be more plastic in the oceans than fish (by weight).

Some situations today are really absurd. For
example, some people sell bananas or peeled
oranges in polystyrene packaging and plastic film.
Nature gives us fruit with natural packaging and
we throw it away and replace it with plastic!

What we can do is this

THE 7 Rs (PLUS ONE MORE)

1. RETHINK

If you're reading this book, it's because you've already started thinking about ocean plastics and you've begun to rethink your habits. That's what the first of the Rs reminds us: we can't go on like this, we have to change!

For example, when we go shopping, we usually only think about the product itself, but we also need to think about the packaging it's in. Other questions to rethink: Do I really need this product? Is there a more environmentally friendly alternative?

2. REFUSE

One of the first things you can do is refuse objects that are not essential. In other words, learn to say "No." The most flagrant example is drinking straws. They are not really necessary, and they represent a huge amount of plastic that will not be recycled and will easily end up in the ocean.

Refuse:

- All types of disposable plastic (glasses, straws, plates)
- Balloons
- Gifts and toys that you don't consider essential
- Products packaged in unnecessary plastic
- Plastic bags
- Plastic water bottles

A tip: People almost always give us these things with the best intentions. So they may be surprised or even offended when we refuse to accept them. If that happens, explain your reasons— with a smile, of course. It works better.

3. REDUCE

This R is obvious, but it may be the one that takes the most work. It's not easy to reduce our use of plastic because it's embedded in almost everything we consume. Often, reducing it means consuming less. And that's difficult when you live in a "consumer society" like ours. I hope you try.

4. REPAIR

Everything around us encourages us to buy new things at every moment! But if we are committed to our ideas, it is easier to change our attitudes. Instead of buying clothes, shoes, toys, and cellphones so often, buy them only when you can no longer repair what you already have. And, of course, buy new things only when you really need them. For example, you can replace the broken glass on your cellphone (instead of rushing out to buy another one) and glue the wobbly sole of your running shoe back on.

Unfortunately, many shops that used to fix things have disappeared, but little by little people have organized themselves to help each other repair their belongings. Check out the Repair Cafés that already exist in many cities.

5. REUSE

If the plastic is already in your hands, try to make it last as long as you can. There are lots of plastic objects and packaging that you can use more than once: plastic bottles, Styrofoam boxes, plastic bags.

It's also possible to use some of the plastic that inevitably comes your way to make artworks, decorations for your room, or objects to help organize your things. There are lots of ideas on the internet, but I'm sure you have lots in your head too!

6. RECYCLE

Many people think that recycling is a perfect and easy way to get rid of plastics. But it's not. Recycling should really be the last resort. We should first try to solve the problem using the other Rs, and only then, if there is no alternative, recycle. The next chapter is devoted to explaining why plastic recycling is far from a perfect solution.

Even so, it is important that we do our part. All plastic packaging must be placed in the proper recycling bin. And remember: don't put toys, pens, appliances, or fuel and oil bottles in recycling bins because they are contaminated and cannot be recycled.

Tip to avoid flying plastic: Put plastic packaging in recycling bins. If the container is full, choose another one nearby or take it home and put it in your own recycling bin.

PERHAPS THE MOST IMPORTANT OF ALL...
7. REVOLUTIONIZE!

It's not enough to change your own habits. Try to get other people and organizations to rethink how they deal with plastics. For example, send messages to your representatives at city hall, to the supermarket chains where you do your shopping, to restaurants and cafés. At your school, talk to your classmates and teacher and see what changes you can make during snack time and at the canteen or cafeteria. See how you can improve the school's recycling program.

What do we do when the cookies that we like so much and that come in four layers of packaging call to us in the aisles of the supermarket? We remember another R—resist!

Recycling: Why Can't We Just Relax?

Recycling has a long way to go

In the past, not only was there less plastic produced and consumed, but its impact on nature was unknown. And the word "recycling" made us feel relaxed. As long as we put plastic packaging in recycling bins, there was no problem. This plastic would be transformed, as if by magic, into other objects. Simple!

Our peace of mind ended when we began to understand all the problems associated with plastics and their recycling.

I invite you to dive into this sea of problems. Plastic problems. Not very pleasant. Can you take it?

THE NUMBERS SHOULD WAKE US UP

In the world today: Only 14% of the plastic produced is collected for recycling, and only about 10% is actually recycled.

In Europe today: Recycling has increased by 80% in the last ten years, but only 41% of plastic packaging is recycled.

In North America today: The United States and Canada recycle only about 9% of their plastic.

Diving into a sea of problems

In many regions of the world, waste management systems and recycling don't exist or don't function properly.

Why not?
Collecting, sorting, treating, and recycling waste costs a great deal of money because it involves technologies and people to operate these systems. This is the main reason why they don't exist or don't function.

Even if they do exist, these systems may not work very well because of lack of investment, disorganization, and/or people still not separating their garbage. In short, environmental problems are not yet a priority for everyone.

As a result, only a part of plastic packaging is recycled—a small or large part, depending on the region of the world.

PROBLEM #2

This is not a problem of your beach. It's a global problem.

Why?
Like so many other environmental problems (such as climate change and air pollution), the problem of plastics in the oceans is a problem without borders. It is not limited to a particular region of the world. Even if plastic comes from a particular region, it quickly travels through ocean currents and is a source of problems all over the planet.

SHIPPING WASTE TO OTHER COUNTRIES

Over the last few decades, countries in North America and Europe have exported large volumes of waste to Asian countries, where the material used to be in demand for making new products. But in 2018, the Chinese government banned the import of such waste, and other Asian countries are beginning to follow suit.

In 2019, for example, the Philippines returned sixty-nine containers of waste from Canada that had been in the Manila port for six years. The waste had been labeled as recyclable plastic, but when it was opened, officials found that two-thirds of the containers were filled with household garbage, including used diapers.

I hope these changes to decades-long practices will force countries to produce and use less plastic and take responsibility for their own garbage.

In front of the Canadian Embassy in Makati City, Philippines, environmental activists lead a protest against illegally shipped containers filled with Canadian garbage.

PROBLEM #3

Recycling is not magic.

Why?

We may think that a piece of plastic packaging placed in a recycling bin will be magically transformed into a new plastic package, without any environmental cost. But that's not how it works. Recycling is not just a matter of melting down a piece of plastic and making a new piece out of it. That's because, first, recycling always involves water and energy consumption. And second, plastic cannot be endlessly recycled—it loses properties every time it goes through the recycling process.

PROBLEM #4

Even in countries where recycling systems are in place, lots of plastic objects and packaging end up in rivers and oceans.

Why?

People are not always careful about the way they dispose of their waste. For example, they often abandon their garbage outside or put it in full bins that end up overflowing. In these cases, the garbage ends up wafting away or being taken by animals. It soon shows up in rivers and oceans.

In addition, many objects end up in the ocean because of the way we use toilets and the ways in which wastewater treatment plants (WWTPs) operate. WWTPs are places where the water that comes from the sewers is treated before it returns to the natural environment.

Let's look at the system step by step.

WWTPs are a great invention because they filter waste and pollutants. However, the system is far from perfect because, in many places, especially in older urban areas, the stormwater drains are still connected to sewage treatment plants. On days when it rains a lot, the treatment plants are overwhelmed by so much water and untreated sewage is discharged directly into bodies of water.

This means that waste from toilets and stormwater drains is no longer filtered by the treatment plants during these periods. Destination: the sea!

PROBLEM #5

Almost 40 percent of the plastic we use is not easily recyclable.

Why not?
There are a number of reasons:

- Some plastic is damaged or contaminated with substances that are dangerous to health.

- Some plastic objects are very small and they are expensive to collect and transport (e.g., straws).

- Some plastic packaging contains materials that are hard to separate (e.g., packaging made of various types of plastic).

In all these cases, recycling is very expensive and unprofitable. So, most of the time, the plastic is not recycled.

Despite these problems, it's crucial that we continue to separate waste and contribute to higher recycling rates.

WHY DOES RECYCLING PLASTIC PRESENT SO MANY CHALLENGES?

Different plastics have different melting points, meaning that some melt at higher temperatures than others. As a result, different types of plastics cannot always be melted together, as they would become very fragile and of no use for making strong packaging.

For example, there are plastics—such as polyethylene and polypropylene—that only bond well with plastics in their own family, because they have a low melting point and do not mix well with plastics with a higher melting point. (For more information on melting points, see page 59.)

To recycle plastics, you must first carefully separate the different types of plastic and only then combine plastics according to the polymer structure of each (for more information, see page 58).

All these operations are expensive and make the process uneconomical.

The result: A large quantity of plastic is hidden "under the rug." It is not recycled, so it either goes to landfill or it is incinerated (burned at a high temperature). These are all bad solutions—first, because plastic does not break down quickly in landfills, and second, because toxic substances are released when plastic is burned.

Pretending the problem doesn't exist...

Dealing with this problem is not easy. So we often choose to stick our heads in the sand and pretend the problem doesn't exist. Then we come up with all sorts of excuses (some pretty lame ones) to deal with it.

1. The planet is huge, nature is powerful, and the planet is indestructible.

Contrary to what many people think, nature is fragile. It's easy to understand why: all the elements of the natural environment are connected and are related to each other. A change in one element has repercussions in the others. The planet has a great capacity to adapt, but there are limits (and we've already exceeded them!).

2. Science and technology invent something new every day!

Contrary to what many people think, technology can't solve all the problems. It cannot produce the oxygen all of us need to breathe, and it doesn't have the ability to regulate the earth's climate. It can't stop millions of tons of plastic from letting off toxic substances in the oceans during the decomposition process or from being swallowed by animals.

3. But aren't businesses concerned about the environment?

Many companies have real environmental concerns and invest in research and new technologies to reduce their impact on the environment and on society. But companies only change when they think that their consumers demand it.

4. I don't need to worry about this because institutions and the government are dealing with the situation.

Governments and institutions choose what to spend money on sometimes based on political pressure from companies, which want to defend their interests and not lose money. And, despite the warnings of scientists, corrective measures are not always taken at the right time or in time.

Alternatives to plastic

Plastic	Alternatives	Why use these alternatives?
Plastic straws	▶ Straws made of aluminum, bamboo, or reusable plastic ▶ Straws made of real straw	Aluminum and bamboo straws can be used over and over. Just wash them and they're ready to use again.
Plastic bags	▶ Reusable bags ▶ Biodegradable bags made with potato starch ▶ Cloth bags ▶ Cardboard boxes	You can carry a reusable bag in your backpack with you wherever you go in case you need to refuse a plastic one.
Disposable plastic bottles	Reusable bottles (canteen type)	You only need one for the rest of your life. Just fill, drink, and refill (and, of course, wash it well from time to time).

Plastic toothbrushes	● Wooden or bamboo toothbrushes ● Brushes in which the bristle part is replaced but the handle is reused	It's a big mystery why, but a lot of toothbrushes appear on beaches. Over time, they break into thousands of little pieces.
Cotton swabs with a plastic stick	Cotton swabs with a stick made of cardboard, pressed paper, bamboo, or wood	They work as well as the plastic ones and break down if they end up in the oceans. But either way, never flush cotton swabs down the toilet.
Balloons	Flower garlands, paper kites, or soap bubbles	They're colorful and festive, and if they do, alas, end up in the sea, they have less of an environmental impact.

Other practical ideas

If we buy food in bulk, we waste less and reduce the plastic. We should try to buy bulk products (beans, grains, rice, fruits, and vegetables) as much as possible. Buy from reliable sources because bulk products don't always have the information about origin and shelf life that usually appears on food packaging labels. Don't forget that packaging has advantages in terms of food safety, which is important.

Use cloth napkins instead of paper ones whenever you can.

Other ideas:

- Buy butter wrapped in vegetal (parchment) paper.

- Avoid buying fish, meat, and fruit packed in polystyrene trays.

- Avoid buying coffee made with disposable pods or tea bags made with plastic (just one bag gives off billions of microplastic particles).

DETERGENTS AND HYGIENE PRODUCTS

In the case of detergents, liquid soaps, and shampoos, try to use packaging that can be refilled, or buy powdered or bar soap instead. Use solid soap and try solid shampoo, which is also available.

Avoid hygiene products that contain plastic microparticles. Look on the labels for polyethylene (PE), polypropylene (PP), and polyethylene terephthalate (PET). They all mean plastic!

CLOTHING

Avoid buying clothes made of synthetics. It is difficult, but it is good to buy fewer and better-quality products. Wash synthetic clothing (especially "polar fleece" materials) less often so that fewer of the microplastics released during washing end up in the sea. Spot-cleaning to remove a small stain is better than washing the whole garment. Special washing bags are also available to retain microplastics and prevent them going to the sea at all.

WATER

Drink tap water rather than bottled water, except in places where treated tap water is not available.

Plastic bottles lie in a heap in a metal cage on a truck in Isla Mujeres, Mexico.

I'm not an alien (I'm a real earthling)

Some people make very funny faces when I refuse to take a plastic cup or a straw. Sometimes, they look at me as if I were an alien. But would an alien worry so much about the earth's oceans?

DEALING WITH OTHER PEOPLE'S MIND-SETS

Expression some people make when I refuse to accept disposable plastic.

Expression people make when they see photos of the tons of plastic floating in the oceans.

Expression most people make when they grasp the enormity of the problem.

Our behavior in relation to the environment is changing as we become more aware. For example, many people used to pee on the streets, spit on the floor, and throw garbage out the car window during their travels! This used to be considered normal, but it's not any longer. Everyone realizes how much more healthy and safe it is to live in a clean environment.

Something similar is happening with plastics. Many people, faced with the consequences plastics have on the environment, are changing their attitudes and inspiring others.

If you meet people who are skeptical or ill-informed about ocean plastics or people who think your position is strange, don't be hostile. Explain calmly what you know and try to make them understand the problem and be willing to change.

I have changed.

I was different before I began to focus on ocean plastics. Often, when I heard about a problem, I would wait for someone else to do something . . .

After a while, I changed my attitude. I thought I should write to the people responsible for the problem. I would write a polite letter to make people aware and explain the consequences. Present alternatives. Share messages. Keep at it. Protest when they do the opposite of what they said they were going to do. I changed.

You can change too!

Good examples

Fortunately, there are lots of good examples of new ways of approaching the ocean plastics problem.

In Finland, a supermarket chain has committed itself to being 100 percent plastic-free on its branded products by 2023, replacing all plastic packaging with cardboard or other fully recyclable materials.

China stopped importing garbage, plastic waste in particular, from other countries in 2018.

In 2016, France became the first country in the world to ban disposable plastic plates, cups, and cutlery. The measure will be implemented in 2020.

In 2019, the European Union banned single-use plastic cutlery, cotton swabs, straws and stirrers, and polystyrene cups. A ban on single-use plastic will come into force in Europe in 2021. Member states will also have to reduce the use of plastic food containers and plastic lids. By 2025, 90 percent of all plastic bottles produced will be collected and recycled.

Canada aims to ban single-use plastics "as early as" 2021.

In the United States, eight states, including California, New York, and Hawaii, have banned single-use plastic bags.

Sweden collects 1.8 billion aluminum cans and plastic bottles every year. In Germany 97–99 percent of nonreusable bottles are returned and the recycling rate for cans is 99 percent. Both countries have special machines in supermarkets where people

can deposit packaging for recycling and receive some money in return.

A number of countries have banned microbeads in cosmetics, including Canada, France, India, Ireland, Italy, the Netherlands, New Zealand, South Africa, Sweden, the United Kingdom, and the United States.

On the island of Bali, in Indonesia, sisters Isabel and Melati Wijsen (ten and twelve years old) organized a big campaign to make Bali plastic-free. Alarmed by the shocking piles of plastic they saw on the island beaches, they got more than 100,000 signatures on a petition and even went on a hunger strike to draw the attention of the local governor.

Many countries have implemented measures to limit the use of plastic bags. In 2008, China banned the free distribution of thin plastic bags (less than one-thousandth of an inch, or 0.025 millimeters) and continues to take steps to reduce their use. Many other countries and regions have done the same, creating taxes on plastic bags or limiting their distribution (e.g., Australia, California, Chile, Kenya).

Scientific laboratories all over the world are looking for sustainable solutions to plastics and their waste disposal. It has been discovered, for example, that some bacteria, larvae, and fungi are able to eat and digest some types of plastic. Another discovery is that enzymes can be manipulated to make them capable of eating bottles made of PET plastic, the most common type of plastic bottle.

PUT THE ECONOMY ON A CIRCULAR PATH

More and more people in industry are talking about an idea called the Circular Economy that could bring about great change.

Nowadays, it is common to extract resources from nature, produce things (shoes, computers, food), and then dispose of waste in a way that is not sustainable. It is often not taken into account that the planet's resources are limited or that nonrenewable energy is being used.

The Circular Economy proposes that industries and businesses become responsible for the waste they generate. As much as possible, materials are reused in production (incorporating materials from recycling), articles are repaired when they are damaged, and products are recycled when their life is over. The idea is that a raw material, when it is extracted from nature, circulates within this circuit for a long, long time, allowing time for nature to regenerate.

A great idea, don't you think?

Create a network

To solve the problem of plastics in the oceans, we need to create a super-team. We need a huge network of people of all ages, in all lines of work, and from all regions of the world. It is a network that includes companies, governments, and associations.

Everyone. Together.

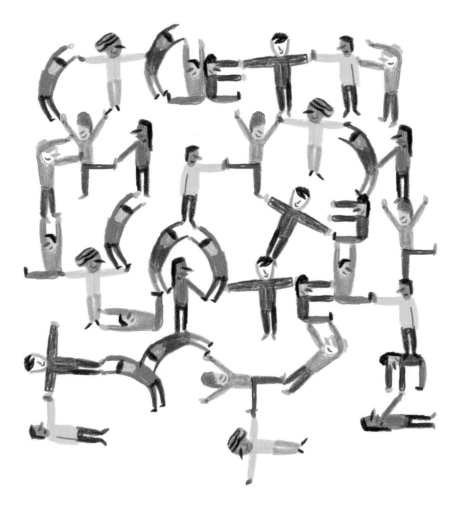

I hope that all of you are willing to roll up your sleeves and get to work. This means refusing to use plastic when it is unnecessary, looking for alternatives to plastic, and being inspired by the good ideas that you come across. There are already many of us working on this issue, but we need an ever-growing network of people in order to get rid of the plastic in the oceans.

Gulf of Mexico, Texas

Floating garbage, Lake Michigan, Chicago

Laysan Albatross looks curiously at a pile of collected lighters, Hawaii

Collected plastic samples, Long Beach, California

Crismina Beach, Portugal, February 2016

Abano Beach, Portugal, June 2016

Guincho Beach, Portugal, October 2016

Avencas Beach, Portugal, March 2018

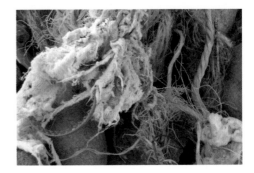

Ana and Balaena plasticus

Balaena plasticus

Hoping to raise awareness about ocean plastics in people of all ages, I worked with nature photographer Luís Quinta to create *Balaena plasticus*. The project was carried out in 2014 with the support of Almada City Council in Portugal.

Balaena plasticus is an installation about 30 feet (10 meters) long. It represents the skeleton of a baleen whale and was built entirely with white plastic objects found on the beach.

Whales are the largest animals on the planet. This one represents one of the biggest problems of our time.

Ana, why do you call pieces of garbage "treasures"?

Hey, that's a good question! Garbage is garbage, of course. And when it has an impact on the environment, of course it's not a treasure. But some pieces of garbage are interesting for their rarity, for the stories they can tell, and for what they reveal about the sea, the currents, erosion, and pollutants. It's in this sense that I sometimes call my findings "treasures."

ACKNOWLEDGMENTS

Catarina Eira

Christopher Kim Pham

Ester Serrão

Gil Penha Lopes

Luís Quinta

Miguel Aranda da Silva

Tanya Mendes Silveira

Tracey Williams

Ana Milhazes Martins, of Zero Waste Portugal, who's a role model for how to live without generating waste

Carolina Saramago, from Feel4Planet

Eunice Maia, from the Maria Granel project, which opened the first plastic-less bulk food store in Portugal

Herberto Figueiredo (Plastik Beach), Gonçalo Silva (Silver Coast Beachcombing), and Silvano Bem (Seamouse), the first beachcombers I met in Portugal

Miguel Lacerda, from the Sea Guardians project

APLM (Associação Portuguesa do Lixo Marinho; Portuguese Marine Litter Association)

Brigada do Mar Association, for doing a great job of cleaning our beaches

Ocean Alive, for its work with the coastal communities of the Sado estuary

To all the other people and associations committed to campaigns to eliminate marine garbage

A very special thanks to Professor Paula Sobral

ANA PÊGO

When she was little, Ana was lucky that she lived right next to the beach. Some people have backyards. Ana had a beach, and that's where she liked to spend most of her time, exploring, walking, thinking.

When the tide was high, she swam and dove into the waves. When the tide was out, she explored the tide pools, walked along the beach, and looked for fossils. She still does the same things today.

Ana never lost her connection with the beach, and it's by the sea that she continues to find the "marine treasures" she uses in her workshops. Now, she's not just teaching about sea urchins, crabs, and anemones, but beings of a different species: plastic.

Her curiosity and interest in the sea didn't change as Ana grew older. She studied marine biology and fisheries at the University of Algarve in Faro, Portugal. She worked in fisheries at the University of Algarve and later as a laboratory technician at the Guia Maritime Laboratory of the Marine and Environmental Sciences Centre in Cascais, Portugal.

She is involved in environmental education projects that combine science and art. She wants to raise people's awareness about the need to conserve the oceans and believes that art helps people make strong connections with the issues. That's why she created the *Plasticus maritimus* project, which is also a Facebook page where she reports on her discoveries.

Ana on Avencas Beach,
Portugal, 1978

RESOURCES

Adopt-a-Beach Programs

Many areas near the Great Lakes or oceans have Adopt-a-Beach programs. Join one, or start your own! A few examples:

Great Lakes: https://greatlakes.org/get-involved/adopt-a-beach/

California: https://www.coastal.ca.gov/publiced/aab/aab1.html

Florida: https://www.volusia.org/services/growth-and-resource-management/environmental-management/get-involved/adopt-a-beach.stml

Algalita

An organization that has been fighting plastic pollution since 1999.

https://algalita.org

Canadian Geographic: 10,000 Changes

Resources for Canadians who want to learn about and help fight the plastics problem.

https://10000changes.ca/en/

Coastal Living: "11 Amazing Organizations Fighting to Save Our Oceans"

Find brief descriptions and links here for

Surfrider Foundation

Ocean Conservancy

5 Gyres Institute

Environmental Defense Fund

Oceana

Bye Bye Plastic Bags (started by Melati and Isabel Wijsen)

Natural Resources Defense Council

Nature Conservancy

Lonely Whale Foundation

Bahamas Plastic Movement

Parley for the Oceans

https://www.coastalliving.com/lifestyle/the-environment/organizations-fighting-to-save-oceans/

National Geographic: "Running List of Action on Plastic Pollution"

Check back here regularly for updates on actions being taken around the world.

https://www.nationalgeographic.com/environment/2018/07/ocean-plastic-pollution-solutions/

Plastic Oceans

Check out the international and Canadian websites for resources and projects.

https://plasticoceans.org
https://plasticoceans.ca

Sea Smart

An organization from Vancouver, British Columbia, offering local programs for kids as well as free resources for educators anywhere.

https://seasmartschool.com

Video poems by Fiona Tinwei Lam

The plastics issue inspires Ana Pêgo to make art, and it also inspires award-winning Vancouver poet Fiona Tinwei Lam (https://fionalam.net). Here are links to two of her video poems, based on visual poems in her book *Odes & Laments*:

Plasticnic (a colorful animated short poetry video)
https://vimeo.com/387883182

Plasticpoems (two unnarrated visual poems that use animated text)
https://vimeo.com/386862235

SOURCES

The Species *Plasticus maritimus*

Tons of plastic into oceans every year (p. 32): Jambeck, J. and coauthors. 2015. Plastic waste inputs from land into the ocean. *Science* 347: 768–771. Available from: https://jambeck.engr.uga.edu/landplasticinput. Accessed September 12, 2019.

More plastic in the sea than fish (p. 32): World Economic Forum, Ellen MacArthur Foundation and McKinsey & Company. 2016. *The New Plastics Economy: Rethinking the Future of Plastics.* Available from: https://www.ellenmacarthurfoundation.org/publications/the-new-plastics-economy-rethinking-the-future-of-plastics. Accessed September 12, 2019.

Plastic far from the coast and at depth (p. 36): Pham, C.K. and coauthors. 2014. Marine litter distribution and density in European seas, from the shelves to deep basins. *PLOS One* 9(4): e95839. Available from: https://journals.plos.org/plosone/article?id=10.1371/journal.pone.0095839. Accessed September 12, 2019.

Time for ocean litter to disintegrate (p. 37): National Oceanic and Atmospheric Administration (NOAA). n.d. Marine debris is everyone's problem [poster]. Available from: https://www.whoi.edu/fileserver.do?id=107364&pt=2&p=88817. Accessed September 24, 2019; Wright, M. and coauthors. 2018. The stark truth about how long your plastic footprint will last on the planet. *Telegraph.* Available from: https://www.telegraph.co.uk/news/2018/01/10/stark-truth-long-plastic-footprint-will-last-planet/. Accessed September 24, 2019.

Microplastics and chemicals (pp. 44, 47): Kershaw, P.J., editor. 2015. *Sources, Fate and Effects of Microplastics in the Marine Environment: A Global Assessment.* Joint Group of Experts on the Scientific Aspects of Marine Environmental Protection (GESAMP). No. 90, 96 p. Available from: https://ec.europa.eu/environment/marine/good-environmental-status/descriptor-10/pdf/GESAMP_microplastics%20full%20study.pdf. Accessed September 12, 2019.

5 Gyres Institute expeditions (p. 48): Eriksen, M. and coauthors. 2014. Plastic pollution in the world's oceans: more than 5 trillion plastic pieces weighing over 250,000 tons afloat at sea. *PLOS One* 9(12): e111913. Available from: https://journals.plos.org/plosone/article/citation?id=10.1371/journal.pone.0111913. Accessed September 12, 2019.

Plastics in freshwater environments (p. 48): Blettler, M.C.M. and coauthors. 2018. Freshwater plastic pollution: recognizing research biases and identifying knowledge gaps. *Water Research* 143: 416–424. Abstract available from: https://www.ncbi.nlm.nih.gov/pubmed/29986250. Accessed September 12, 2019.

Microplastics in tap water (p. 49): Tyree, C. and D. Morrison. 2017. *Invisibles: The Plastic Inside Us.* Available from: https://orbmedia. org/stories/Invisibles_plastics/. Accessed September 12, 2019.

Microplastics in bottled water (p. 49): Mason, S.A. and coauthors. 2018. Synthetic polymer contamination in bottled water. *Frontiers in Chemistry* 6: 407. Available from: https://www.ncbi.nlm.nih.gov/ pmc/articles/PMC6141690/. Accessed September 12, 2019.

Plastic entering the Great Lakes every year (pp. 50–51): Hoffman, M.J. and C. Tyler. 2018. Tons of plastic trash enter the Great Lakes every year—where does it go? *The Conversation.* Available from: https:// theconversation.com/tons-of-plastic-trash-enter-the-great-lakes-every- year-where-does-it-go-100423. Accessed September 12, 2019.

Plastic in the soil (p. 51): de Souza Machado, A.A. and coauthors. 2018. Microplastics as an emerging threat to terrestrial ecosystems. *Global Change Biology* 24(4): 1405–1416. Available from: https://doi.org/10.1111/ gcb.14020. Accessed October 14, 2019; Boots, B. and coauthors. 2019. Effects of microplastics in soil ecosystems: above and below ground. *Environmental Science and Technology* 53(19): 11496–11506. Available from: https://doi.org/10.1021/acs.est.9b03304. Accessed October 14, 2019.

Do You Want to Know More about Plastic?

2019, Production and disposal of plastic uses almost 14% of oil and gas (p. 57): Vidal, J. 2020. The plastic polluters won 2019— and we're running out of time to stop them. *The Guardian.* Available from: https://www.theguardian.com/environment/2020/jan/02/year- plastic-pollution-clean-beaches-seas. Accessed January 23, 2020.

2020, Governments and corporations commit to reduced production of plastic (p. 57): Vidal, J. 2020. The plastic polluters won 2019—and we're running out of time to stop them. *The Guardian*. Available from: https://www.theguardian.com/environment/2020/jan/02/year-plastic-pollution-clean-beaches-seas. Accessed January 23, 2020.

Where the world's plastic is produced (p. 62): d'Ambrières, W. 2019. Plastics recycling worldwide: current overview and desirable changes. *Journal of Field Actions* 19: 12–21. Available from: https://journals.openedition.org/factsreports/5102. Accessed September 12, 2019.

Common Ocean Plastic

International Coastal Cleanup data (p. 66): Ocean Conservancy. Cleanup Reports. Available from: https://oceanconservancy.org/trash-free-seas/international-coastal-cleanup/annual-data-release/. Accessed September 12, 2019.

Origins of marine debris (p. 67): United Nations Educational, Scientific and Cultural Organization (UNESCO). 2017. Facts and figures on marine pollution. Available from: http://www.unesco.org/new/en/natural-sciences/ioc-oceans/focus-areas/rio-20-ocean/blueprint-for-the-future-we-want/marine-pollution/facts-and-figures-on-marine-pollution/. Accessed September 12, 2019; Kershaw, P.J., editor. 2015. *Sources, Fate and Effects of Microplastics in the Marine Environment: A Global Assessment*. Joint Group of Experts on the Scientific Aspects of Marine Environmental Protection (GESAMP). No. 90, 96 p. Available from: http://www.gesamp.org/publications/reports-and-studies-no-90. Accessed September 12, 2019.

Cigarette butts tossed on the ground each year (p. 68): A Greener Future. n.d. The cigarette butt cycle [infographic]. Available from: https://www.agreenerfuture.ca/the-butt-blitz. Accessed September 12, 2019.

Water bottles bought and recycled (p. 70): Laville, S. and M. Taylor. 2017. A million bottles a minute: world's plastic binge 'as dangerous as climate change.' *The Guardian*. Available from: https://www.theguardian.com/environment/2017/jun/28/a-million-a-minute-worlds-plastic-bottle-binge-as-dangerous-as-climate-change. Accessed September 12, 2019.

Plastic bag found in the Mariana Trench (p. 71): Chiba, S. and coauthors. 2018. Human footprint in the abyss: 30 year records of deep-sea plastic debris.

Marine Policy 96: 204–212. Available from: https://www.sciencedirect.com/science/article/pii/S0308597X17305195#. Accessed September 12, 2019.

Bans on use of plastic bags (p. 71): Excell, C. 2019. 127 countries now regulate plastic bags. Why aren't we seeing less pollution? World Resources Institute. Available from: https://www.wri.org/blog/2019/03/127-countries-now-regulate-plastic-bags-why-arent-we-seeing-less-pollution. Accessed September 12, 2019.

Straws used in Europe every year (p. 77): Darrah, C. 2017. *Leverage Points for Reducing Single-use Plastics*. Background report for Seas at Risk. Available from: https://seas-at-risk.org/24-publications/800-single-use-plastic-and-the-marine-environment.html. Accessed September 12, 2019.

Exotic Ocean Plastic

Products transported by boat (p. 94): United Nations Conference on Trade and Development (UNCTAD). 2013. *Review of Maritime Transport 2012*. UNCTAD/RMT/2012. Available from: https://unctad.org/en/pages/publications/Review-of-Maritime-Transport-(Series).aspx. Accessed September 12, 2019.

Shipping containers transported in 2017, and the number that fell into the sea from 2008 to 2016 (p. 94): World Shipping Council. *Containers Lost at Sea—2017 Update*. Available from: http://www.worldshipping.org/industry-issues. Accessed September 12, 2019.

What We Can Do

Estimated date of more plastic in the oceans than fish (p. 116): World Economic Forum, Ellen MacArthur Foundation and McKinsey & Company. 2016. *The New Plastics Economy: Rethinking the Future of Plastics*. Available from: https://www.ellenmacarthurfoundation.org/publications/the-new-plastics-economy-rethinking-the-future-of-plastics. Accessed September 12, 2019.

Recycling: Why Can't We Just Relax?

Plastic collected for recycling and actually recycled (p. 125): World Economic Forum, Ellen MacArthur Foundation and McKinsey & Company. 2016. *The*

New Plastics Economy: Rethinking the Future of Plastics. Available from: https://www.ellenmacarthurfoundation.org/publications/the-new-plastics-economy-rethinking-the-future-of-plastics. Accessed September 12, 2019.

Recycling rates in Europe (p. 125): Plastics Europe. 2018. *Plastics—the Facts 2018.* Available from: https://www.plasticseurope.org/en/resources/publications. Accessed September 12, 2019.

Recycling rates in North America (p. 125): Environment and Climate Change Canada. 2019. *Economic Study of the Canadian Plastic Industry, Markets and Waste.* Available from: http://publications.gc.ca/collections/collection_2019/eccc/En4-366-1-2019-eng.pdf. Accessed September 24, 2019; U.S. Environmental Protection Agency. *Facts and Figures about Materials, Waste and Recycling. Plastics: Material-Specific Data.* n.d. Available from: https://www.epa.gov/facts-and-figures-about-materials-waste-and-recycling/plastics-material-specific-data. Accessed September 24, 2019.

Tea bags made with plastic (p. 138): Hernandez, L.M. and coauthors. 2019. Plastic teabags release billions of microparticles and nanoparticles into tea. *Environmental Science and Technology* 53(21): 12300–12310. Available from: https://doi.org/10.1021/acs.est.9b02540. Accessed October 14, 2019.

PHOTO CREDITS

All photos © Ana Pêgo, except for those noted below.

50 plastic waste floating in Lake Erie © wilgory / iStockphoto.com; **62** plastic resin pellets © aydinmutlu / iStockphoto.com; **63** veterinarian prepares to clean an oiled Kemp's ridley sea turtle © NOAA and Georgia Department of Natural Resources; **129 top** environmental activists, Philippines © Pacific Press Agency / Alamy Stock Photo; **bottom** heap of waste © meaduva / Flickr.com; **139** plastic bottles in metal cage © Eddy Galeotti / Alamy Stock Photo; **148 top** trash collected on coastal beach © inga spence /Alamy Stock Photo; **bottom** garbage floating on Lake Michigan © stevegeer / iStockphoto.com; **149 top** albatross looks at pile of disposable lighters © National Ocean Service, National Oceanic and Atmospheric Administration; **bottom** collected plastic samples © Citizen of the Planet / Alamy Stock Photo; **156** Ana and *Balaena plasticus* © Luís Quinta

AUTHOR AND ILLUSTRATOR BIOS

Ana Pêgo is a marine biologist and award-winning artist whose plastic artworks have been exhibited internationally. She has led environmental education projects that combine science and art, providing workshops to school-aged children and initiating the *Plasticus maritimus* project, which raises awareness about the impacts of plastic on our oceans. She lives near Lisbon, Portugal.

Bernardo P. Carvalho is a prize-winning illustrator and co-founder of Planeta Tangerina. He lives near Lisbon, Portugal.

Isabel Minhós Martins is an award-winning author and co-founder of acclaimed publisher Planeta Tangerina. She lives near Lisbon, Portugal.

Jane Springer is a translator, editor, and author of *Genocide*, a Groundwork Guide. She contributed North American content to the book. She lives in Toronto.

DAVID SUZUKI INSTITUTE

The David Suzuki Institute is a non-profit organization founded in 2010 to stimulate debate and action on environmental issues. The Institute and the David Suzuki Foundation both work to advance awareness of environmental issues important to all Canadians.

We invite you to support the activities of the Institute. For more information please contact us at:

David Suzuki Institute
219 – 2211 West 4th Avenue
Vancouver, BC V6K 4S2
info@davidsuzukiinstitute.org
604-742-2899
www.davidsuzukiinstitute.org

Cheques can be made payable to The David Suzuki Institute.